Modern Sports Karate

Rudolf Jakhel

Modern Sports Karate

Basics of
Techniques and Tactics

Meyer & Meyer Sport

Original title: Modernes Sport Karate - Technische und taktische Grundlagen
First Edition published by the General German University Sports Association
(Allgemeiner Deutscher Hochschulsportverband) Text series „Sports and Learning", No. 12
Hans Putty Verlag, Wuppertal 1989, Germany
Second Edition: 1997 by Meyer & Meyer Verlag, Aachen, Germany

English translation made after the Slovenian edition by Zvone Vodnik, New Zealand
Translation edited by Scott Palmer, United States of America
Final edition by James Beachus, Düsseldorf, Germany

British Library Cataloguing in Publication Data
A catalogue record for this book is available from the British Library

Jakhel, Rudolf:
Modern sports karate: basics of techniques and tactics/
2nd Ed.– Oxford : Meyer & Meyer Sport (UK) Ltd., 2000
ISBN 1-84126-042-8

© 1998 by Meyer & Meyer Sport (UK) Ltd.
2nd Edition 2000
Oxford, Aachen, Olten (CH), Vienna, Québec, Lansing/Michigan, Adelaide,
Auckland, Johannesburg, Budapest
Member of the World
Sportpublishers' Association
Cover photo: Bongarts Sportfotografie GmbH, Hamburg
All photograps by the author exept the following:
1-4, 8, 9, 13, 14a/b (T. Nett), 7 (F. Joch), 10 (H. Müller),
Illustrations with antique drawings with permission of the author from:
4000 Selbstverteidigung (4000 Years of Self-defense)
by Michael Baranyai-Bodorfalva, Rerosh-Amtmann, Wien 1989, second edition.
The illustration of a Greek vase with the permission of the author from:
Vom Zweikampf (On Duel), by Keith R. Kernspecht
Wu-Shu-Verlag, Kernspecht, Burg/Fehmarn 1992, third revised edition
Cover design: Birgit Engelen, Stolberg
Cover exposure: frw, Reiner Wahlen, Aachen
Type exposure: Pre Print Service, Michael Hesterkamp, Aachen
Printed and bound in Germany
by Druckpunkt Offset GmbH, Bergheim
ISBN 1-84126-042-8
e-mail: verlag@meyer-meyer-sports.com

54

Early forms of European karate-like fighting

One of the drawings from a series on free fighting made 1512 by the famous medieval painter Albrecht Dürer. The defender is applying a reverse or diametrical thrust front kick.

3. APPLICATION OF THE FIGHTING REPERTOIRE IN SPORTS KARATE

SPORT & LERNEN

Schriftenreihe im H. Putty Verlag
ALLGEMEINER DEUTSCHER HOCHSCHULSPORTVERBAND

**Modernes
Sport-Karate**

Rudolf Jakhel

Review of the book
MODERN SPORTS KARATE
by Rudolf Jakhel.

Since it doesn't depend on the Japanese teaching forms, this book is a refreshing change from "regular" karate books. Jakhel successfully undertakes an already long overdue attempt to analyze the subject of training in karate with Western know-how and Western logic. This is a welcome approach, because it makes the learning process faster and more efficient when the way the lessons are laid out is similar to one's own thought and learning process.

Usually, the teaching forms presented in karate books depend on the Japanese karate philosophy and thus don't correspond with the European, analytical way of thinking.

The way in which Jakhel presents his material should be encouraged because it contributes to the emancipation of Europe from Japan and helps it to reach its true limit of performance in sports karate.

One must delve into all the varying levels of the sport in order to be able to carry out a thorough examination, which can be used to analyze and check the methods of teaching. This is the only way of transferring experience from other branches of sport into karate – which has happened in this book – so that optimum performance by the athlete is encouraged. In this way, one can establish a broad basis for sports karate in which there is no longer any need to refer to the Japanese culture when one wishes to learn karate. The Western student's own cultural roots are enough.

This book offers a complete, easy to understand, and detailed explanation of sports karate. It is to be welcomed as a contribution to a trend which has been developing for some time now. The book's analytical, European mode of dealing with karate has recently appeared on the agenda of some sports science congresses, and has also been taken into use by competent trainers. This is the context of Jakhel's book.

Dr. Elke von Oehsen

"hochschulsport" (University Sport)
Journal of the General German University Sports Union
Year 17, No 12/1990

PREFACE TO THE ENGLISH-LANGUAGE EDITION

Motto:
*"Times change,
the world changes,
and obviously martial arts
have to change too."*

Gichin Funakoshi,
founder of karate sport

At first, a reader of this book might be shocked by its unusual approach to karate. Karate circles around the globe are generally accustomed to karate that has been coated and permeated with the philosophic religious traditions of the Far East. This gives karate an exotic flavor and keeps it out of reach of a thorough examination by means of any rational, logical analysis usually common in the West. However, only by using such a rational approach was it possible in this book to gain a new, enlightened view of karate as a sport.

DR. ELKE VON OEHSEN's review of this book (repeated on the opposite page) expresses this extremely well. Her wholeheartedly positive evaluation lends a special weight for two reasons. Firstly, she is a black belt fourth degree in wadoryu, one of the traditional karate styles, as well as author and co-author of several karate books. Her recognition of the correctness and usefulness of an explanation, which abandons traditional grounds, is so unusual in classic karate, that this by itself is of extraordinary importance. Secondly, the reviewer is not only a high ranking karate black belt, but also a researcher in sports science with a doctoral dissertation in karate. The combination of these two top qualifications probably makes her one of the most competent experts in the field of karate. Dr. von Oehsen's evaluation of this book is also unlike a normal critique – it is a valuable appraisal of the neutral and overlapping approach depicted in this book.

As I explain in the next chapter (Introduction to the first German edition), this book is an interim report on a development project "Rationalization in Karate Sport." Since its first publication, further knowledge has been gained, and the sections on the instruction of karate have been made simpler due to several improvements in the methods. However, the latest innovations have been only partially considered in this edition. This book is limited to the presentation of a

9

sports-oriented repertoire of fighting actions, their rationale, and their technical and tactical structure, as well as the possibilities for their application. How one learns this sports karate repertoire systematically, step by step, could only have been superficially touched on in this book. To go further demands yet more specialized and comprehensive work. The problem field of didactics in karate is an extensive and very much misunderstood subject, which at the same time remains blurred because of the innumerable overlapping interests.

When I wrote the book, my students wanted to have all things said without the book becoming too lengthy. The consequence of considering both requirements at the same time has been that the text is highly condensed. It therefore requires rather concentrated reading, as do most reference books. However, the text is meaningfully organized and substantially supported by photographs. Some chapters consist mostly or exclusively of photographs with corresponding explanations. Thus, readers can either work from front to back or dip into the book at random.

The book is also furnished with some illustrations which have no direct relation to the text. There are drawings from the European Middle-Ages and Antiquity. These drawings bear witness that – contrary to the prevailing belief – the Far East wasn't the only cradle of today's popular martial arts. There seem to have existed ample Western and Near Eastern versions, as well as other roots and pre-forms of karate-like fighting, to which we should actually pay more attention.

The way this book looks at karate is broadly consistent with the general aspiration to gain Olympic status for the sport. This step, which has been a long aspiration in karate circles, will certainly herald a new period in the development of karate as a sport. Karate has been systematically transplanted from Japan to Europe and other continents starting from the mid-1950s. That means that it has been developing as a global sport for forty years already – which is longer than the period when it was an exclusively Japanese sport (1920s–1950s). No global sport can depend on specific regional traditions, except in parts, where those traditions correspond with generally valid values, norms, modes of conduct, and ways of thinking. Once karate becomes an Olympic discipline, the general worldwide accepted way of reasoning will, gradually but unavoidably, come to the forefront also in this traditional sport. This book is meant to be a contribution to such a development.

Summer 1997   R. Jakhel

INTRODUCTION TO THE FIRST (GERMAN) EDITION (revised)

Today, more than 40 years since the introduction of karate into the Federal Republic of Germany, there is a multitude of karate books on the market. One might almost think that the subject of "karate" had been exhausted, so that it would be virtually impossible to say something new about it.[1]

This book, however, presents a new approach to karate and explains karate in an unusual way. Its unconventionality comes from the author's aim of writing a karate book which is thoroughly practical and something more than a text book. This book is practical in more ways than one:

1. It focuses entirely on the sports bout *(jiyu-kumite)* as the field of practice in sports karate. It deals only with the actions which are actually used in the sports bout. The fighting techniques and tactics, presented here, have evolved from many years of observation of what most contestants use in sports fighting. It elaborates on the actual patterns of behavior and movement applied by the vast majority of participants in sports contests, regardless of what each of them had to learn in order to obtain his/her belt. The actual sports bout, where karate is applied and thus tested, is both the source and the aim of this book. It is an attempt to illuminate and systematically explain the actual practical and sporting competitive features of karate.[1]

2. The concepts illustrated in this book are based on the realization that the movements and actions in karate have distinct similarities with other types of sports. We have in mind those kinds of sports that include starts (as in the sprint), throwing (as in the shot-put or the javelin), thrusts (as in fencing), hits (as in tennis), kicks (as in soccer), as well as turns, whirls, and jumps (as in gymnastics and figure skating). If such a fact is agreed – unfortunately not at all often the case in karate circles – then a radical change will begin to take place. With this in mind one can begin to apply the analysis of the movements using kinesiology – a science that studies forms and laws of human movements. Thus, the interpretation of karate actions included in this book are based on the "morphologic" characteristics of these actions.[2]

3. The descriptions of karate actions in this book are so comprehensively explained, that everyone wishing to try to learn the karate movements or improve his or her performance can use it. Only one thing has been intentionally omitted: the description of how to hold the hands and feet when hitting the various vital points. When hands and feet are used for this purpose, we call them *impact parts*, because they cause an impact (i.e. a striking impulse), which is the very intent of attack in karate. Until now I have hardly seen a karate book that does not describe the holding of the impact parts. It does not make any sense to repeat that information here. Those unfamiliar with such details can learn them from any of the known karate books, or look carefully at the individual figures in this book.

4. The language used in this book for describing individual karate actions is a pragmatic, everyday language enriched with some expressions from other sports and kinesiology, while some other expressions have been created anew or have been given a special meaning. Where necessary, I have also added (in brackets) the corresponding Japanese expressions as they are generally used in karate. They do not necessarily fit completely, but in this way, traditional karatekas can more easily follow the discussion. For easier reading, I have also used abbreviations consisting of numbers and letters. Coding not only shortens the naming of karate actions but also reveals the patterns of the interrelationship between each of them.[3]

5. The repertoire of fighting actions is not just simply an enumeration and categorization of particular examples of those used in the fighting bout. An extensive systematization is required to illustrate the relativity of the fighting actions with each other, and this demands also a particularly practical layout for the book. They are arranged to give a transparent, logical and comprehensible system, also called the *sports fighting system*. This is based on six types of foot attacks. These, in turn, combine with various *reverse* (diagonal, diametrical, opposite-sided) or *straight* (same-, one-, or single-sided, unilateral) hand attacks to produce a further twelve basic types of combinations. Dependent on which side of the body is used to carry out each of the attack variations, as well as on the varying tactical requirements, there is almost an infinite number of potential variations that can be taught and learned in accordance with well established didactic principles: (a) from known to unknown, (b) from simple to complex, (c) from easy to difficult, and (d) from universal to specific.

6. This book not only gives a systematic review of the basic actions in sports bouts, but also how it is applied. This review consists of three parts. The first part starts with the very concept of sports karate, focusing especially on sports ethics, sports contests and sports training. The essential features of the sports fighting repertoire include karate actions, which have been selected from the inherent logic of the fighting pattern of a sports bout. They are determined on the one

hand by the characteristics of the sports bout and on the other by the general requirement to maximize the effectiveness of the training process. In the second part, we analyze separately the technical and the tactical components of the sports fighting repertoire. Considering the kinetic similarity of karate to other sports, we explain first the phases of the motion cycles from which the combined foot-hand karate attacks have been developed. Following on, the concept of tactics in a karate sports bout is discussed, starting with the situational notion of a *tactical moment*. Tactics are classified as either "passive and preventive" or "active and offensive". The third part covers the possibilities for the practical application of the fighting repertoire. To do this, it analyzes the actual course of a sports bout. We present the most typical variations of attacks and counter-attacks, and also explain advanced variations such as series, specialties, and jump attacks.

Those who are already familiar with sports fighting will soon realize that the majority of technical details in the depicted fighting system are commonly known. Indeed this fact is the starting point of this book: it is not necessary to re-invent something that is already in use. New in this connection in this book, however, is a systematic and comprehensive presentation of the prevailing motion pattern that is generally used in sports bouts, a pattern into which all the varieties of actions can fit. Thus we have created a transparent, meaningful system of fighting combinations derived from (a) a distillation of the multitude of useful actions ranging down to the essential, technically pure form, and (b) a rational systematization which follows the principles of human kinetics. Such a system makes complex motions in karate both easier for the instructor to teach and easier for the student to learn. Similarly, a tactical system has been developed here as well. In karate literature generally, the complex yet utterly practical question of tactics is only ever sparsely touched on.[4] In contrast, this book discerns between and defines the basic tactical notions and categories of the karate sports bout, and systematically elaborates on them.

Because of my commitment to the practice of sports fighting, I have avoided the inclusion of a plethora of highly philosophical concepts that traditionally constitute a part of karate. The culture of the Far East is rich and precious. It does not deserve to be misrepresented by using superficial statements and arbitrarily selected quotations, distorted and thus weakened, as is too often the case in Western karate. As one of the youngest sports, transplanted to the West from the cultural circles of the Far East, first and foremost, karate needs to be thoroughly and rationally examined as well as conceptually and methodically rearranged in order to become adjusted to our way of thinking. Let us remind all those, who think of so-called "traditional" features of karate as being an untouchable heritage, that karate has already once before undergone an all-encompassing cultural adjustment which meant a change of its characteristic traits. Karate, in the form we know it today in the West, was developed from the secret, legend-shrouded martial art of Okinawa, accessible to only a few of the initiated, into a worldwide popular sport only after an excessive Japanization.

The first decisive step towards the spreading of karate around the world was made by the master GICHIN FUNAKOSHI, also named SHOTO, regarded by many as the father of present day karate. This step occurred in 1922 when he published in Japan the first book on karate and triggered its acculturation process. In Japan, karate was soon enormously popular and in the same decade became officially recognized. The question is whether this would have happened as fast had master Funakoshi not fundamentally reformed his Okinawan martial art. In the endeavor to make it more acceptable for the Japanese school system, he japanized his Okinawan martial art and, at the same time, transformed it into a new sport. This he achieved through several measures (not necessarily in the following order), as he:

- transformed the Japanese characters for "karate" from the original meaning "Chinese hand" into the new meaning "empty hand";
- accomplished a "reform of nomenclature", as he himself put it, by exchanging the Okinawan terminology, which was unintelligible to the Japanese, with a corresponding Japanese terminology;
- organized karate training as a schooling system by introducing student's grades and master's degrees (*kyu* and *dan*), as well as by formalizing the requirements for passing into higher grade training classes (e.g., receiving belt grades);
- substantially simplified and shortened katas (forms).[5]

In his last book, written in 1956 (one year before his death), he explained his unambiguous view on the further evolution of karate. His message substantiates the reforms he introduced and makes them totally understandable, leaving no room for misinterpretation. *"Times change, the world changes, and obviously martial arts must change too!"* [6] In the conclusion of the same book, Funakoshi gave himself the future task of popularizing karate in the West. If he had lived long enough to do it himself, we could rightfully presume that he would have done something similar to what he had done for the Japanization of karate. No doubt, he would have invested the maximum effort, and, through further reforms, made karate more suitable to our Western way of thinking.

In Japan, this new sport has continued to develop. From the mid 1930s onward, a new form of proving one's fighting abilities had been slowly evolving – karate sports fighting (jap.: *jiyu kumite*). The final step in the institutionalization of karate sports fighting was the first All-Japanese Karate Championship in 1957. After that, karate became equal to other sports popular in the West. However, in its nature, its substance, methods, and group dynamics as well as language, it has remained essentially Japanese.[7] A deliberate, all-encompassing Westernization or Europeanization of this Far Eastern martial art has never been attempted. So we deal today in European and other Western countries with a relatively widespread sport, which in turn depends on Far Eastern traditions that are not and cannot be properly understood by the vast majority of students.

Confusion about karate remains widespread, mainly because of the fact that it does not exist just as one karate sport, but as a multitude of styles or schools, each one claiming to represent the true concept of karate – even though they are unable to prove it comprehensively. There is a big attraction for Western youth to take up karate. However, this enthusiasm is based more on the exoticism of karate and a touch of the mysticism, that has remained from its pre-sport times, than on its characteristics as a sport. Because of the absence of the Western way of thinking and clear explanations, as well as the corresponding build-up of training methods, the initial enthusiasm of a beginner all too often becomes a frustration; on average, only one out of 200 to 300 beginners will achieve a black belt (master level) degree, and this is where his/her sports career would only just begin.[8]

This book is designed as a contribution towards a clearer explanation of karate. It represents an interim result of an ongoing development project on rationalization in karate sport. This project began in 1971, when I established a karate group at the Institute of Physical Education (later named the Institute of Sports Science) at the University of Technology in Aachen, Germany, and took over the mentorship of a group of sport students who majored in karate. There, I was confronted with a problem which concerns the core of sportsmanship in karate. Many students joined the group who had already been practicing one of the many karate styles and wanted to return to those styles after completing their studies. Consequently, a discussion surged within the group members, which can be summarized in two contemporary areas of questions:

1) Is it proper, for the purpose of teaching karate at an academic level in an institution of sports science, to select only one of the traditional methods of training, about which one cannot or may not ask rational questions? If so, which criteria does one choose to select the right method? Or, in order to be fair, does one have to have as many karate groups as there are karate styles?

2) How can one make the training program general, and yet more intensive, so that when the students have left the institution, they will be able to join some karate club or other, irrespective of the style practised in it, and be able to carry on without any difficulty in adapting, and without giving up the sport?

The answer to these questions is twofold: (a) focusing the training on the fighting bout and (b) the application of kinesiology in the absence of a general theoretical basis in karate. Using this theory, the group developed a new, rational approach to karate, and the teaching and training of karate at the University of Aachen improved from term to term. For some time now, members of our group have practised this book's neutrally-styled fighting repertoire, learning the sport

15

bout system. The same method has been in use also by many other university groups and karate clubs in Germany and abroad.

The fighting system presented here has had many 'co-producers'. During my 30 years or more of involvement in karate in Germany, the United States and other countries, I have come into contact with many karate teachers and contestants who, intentionally or unintentionally, have influenced me with their viewpoints and opinions, their ways of fighting or with both. All of them have been to a certain degree participating in the creation of this fighting repertoire, though it is clear that they will not necessarily agree with all of the presentations and conclusions in this book. Let me mention at least the most important ones among them.

My first teacher in Stuttgart, Germany, was master VLADO SCHMIDT, with whom in 1968 I began to learn my first steps and punches in *jujutsu* and karate self-defense. The enthusiasm he inspired in me still burns today. Following this I spent two years in my home country, Slovenia, where DR. EMIN TOPIC from Zagreb, Croatia, familiarized me with several karate styles: *shotokan*, *shitoryu*, *shukokai*, and *sankukai*. Under his tutelage, I did not merely learn efficient sports fighting – winning prizes at national, federal, and international level – I also gained a valuable attitude towards karate, free of any traditional encumbrances.

Back in those days some independent grand masters of karate also influenced my thoughts strongly. The late ARTHUR HISATAKE (*kyokushinkai*), living at that time in Munich, Germany, commented on some of my observations and gave me much-appreciated guidance. Regrettably, he left us much too early. In addition, the pioneering analytical contributions of CHOJIRO TANI (*shukokai*), and YOSHINAO NAMBU (then *sankukai*) enlightened me on the way karate had been developing.

Three more people greatly influenced my personal development in karate, even though they were never my coaches. The first is ALBRECHT PFLÜGER, one of the pioneers of German karate, with his book on karate which was published about that time.[9] In those days, in regions where there were not many karate teachers, this book fulfilled the function of providing important guidance and information for the karate students of my generation. The second is ZARKO MODRIC from Zagreb, Croatia, master of karate and aikido, who at that time was a correspondent for the *Black Belt* magazine. Through him, I gained an insight into the history of karate and the international karate scene in general. The third is DR. KURT MEINEL of Berlin, Germany, who will be hardly known by many students. Dr. Meinel is a research scientist in physical education who published a comprehensive book on the components and laws of human movement – a reference book that is used widely still today by researchers into this specialty. He is recognized as one of the founders of pedagogical kinesiology. His master book [10] gave me an understanding and comprehension unusual in karate circles. From him, I learned how to analyze the basic kinesiological categories and finally became able to explain to myself the structure of movements in karate actions regarding their mutual interdependence and relationship.

My sports colleagues, with whom I undertook many different things during my first stay in Germany 1971–1976, must also be mentioned. At that time I was a contestant, coach, federal referee and special adviser to the technical commission of the Karate Section in the German Judo Union – then the strongest official karate federation in the country. I refer especially to my sports friends of the Budo Club Nipon Hamburg, led at that time by REINHARD KUBISCH. With its successes in contests and its unorthodox training methods, this karate group had visibly influenced the course of events in the German karate sport. I would also like to mention the federal coaches BERNHARD GOETZ, WOLFGANG ZIEBART and the present federal coach GUENTHER MOHR, as well as the late †RICHARD SCHERER, who was a top German karate fighter. My observation of the way they, and other sports colleagues, who can not all be mentioned here by name, move and fight, has indirectly helped in creating the fighting system presented here.

Many members or ex-members of the karate group at the University of Technology in Aachen, Germany, as well as colleagues in many different university groups and karate clubs in Germany and abroad have co-operated and assisted me in the production of this book. To all of them, I give special thanks. Especially to the ex-coach of the karate group at the UT Aachen, Dr. Konstantin Mavrommatis, 3rd DAN; and further, to Zvone Vodnik, 4th DAN (New Zealand); Ed Weber, 3rd DAN (Luxemburg); Tassos Kamaritsas, 3rd DAN (Greece); Fahri Mahalla, 5th DAN (Switzerland); Karl Skrabl, 4th DAN (Switzerland); Silvo Maric, 4th DAN (Slovenia); Franko Kenda, 4th DAN (Slovenia); Thomas Kubicka, 3rd DAN (Germany); Dr. Kamal Bdair, 2nd DAN (Israel); Dr. Reiner Huba, 2nd DAN (Germany); Dr. Manfred Arnold, 2nd DAN (Germany); Dr. Norbert Koster, 1st DAN (Germany); Dr. Andreas Neuss, 1st DAN (Germany); Dr. Apostolos Kontogeorgakos, 1st DAN (Cyprus); Dr. Georg Kidas, 1st DAN (Greece), and many others. Special thanks goes of course to the Institute of Sports Science and its ex-directors Professor Dr. Günther Luschen and Professor Dr. Franz Müller – for continuous support and free access to the library as well as assistance with taking photos.

Any research work does not end – as this one has not – with the publishing of a report. Any constructive criticism and encouragement will be welcome.

Autumn 1988, revised Summer 1997

Rudolf Jakhel

An ancient Greek vase depicting a scene with the initial fighting stance

Early forms of European karate-like fighting

Contrary to prevailing opinion, Europe possesses its own rich roots in combat sports. The ideas, that came to Europe under exotic names from the Far East, had been known about already in ancient Egyptian and Greek times. These authentic traditions were, in many ways, taken over by the medieval European teachers of fencing and wrestling – as documented in numerous books and drawings from that time. Some historians consider that there is some truth in the thesis, that the Asiatic early form of what we recognize today as karate, was developed from the influences of freestyle fighters of ALEXANDER THE GREAT. These fighters had served in the Macedonian military units, which remained behind in the occupied or newly founded cities of Northern India around 325 B.C. The Japanese Grandmaster MATSUTATSU OYAMA – the founder of the world-wide established karate-style kyokushinkai, – who admired the ancient Greek freestyle fighters, and fought with bulls after their pattern, also favored this thesis. (cf., K. R. Kernspecht, Vom Zweikampf – On Duel, Wu Shu Verlag (Publishers) Kernspecht, 1992). The stance of the two fighters depicted on this ancient Greek vase is astonishingly similar to the well known nekoashi-dachi cat-leg stance in traditional Japanese karate. But as we see, the ancient Greek fighters adopted this stance already several hundreds of years earlier.

1. THE MAIN CHARACTERISTICS OF SPORTS KARATE

THE SPORTING ELEMENTS OF KARATE

For some time now, we have seen a differentiation occurring between karate as a "martial art" and karate as a combat sport. Without entering into any discussion on the declared spiritual goals and dimensions of karate, we can most easily describe the difference between the two by focusing on the technical and tactical goals of each. The technical and tactical goal of karate, as a martial art, is the ability to defend oneself, i.e., prepare to give battle. On the other hand, the technical and tactical goal of karate as a sport is the ability to take part in sporting bouts. In the first instance it is a question of consequentially defending oneself irrespective of the effect this will have on the attacker. Sports karate is about the practical testing of one's fighting capability, whereby the opponents mutually protect each other from injuries in accordance with rules.[11] Consequently, one can conclude that the repertoire of the fighting techniques and tactics applied in karate sports bouts is limited and therefore more specialized than in a real fight without rules. This is the very essence of the difference, and the start point of the discussion in this book.

It is a well-known fact that to try to provide a universally accepted definition of sport will always create difficulties. For our purposes, however, it will be enough if we simply lay down that sport is a socially institutionalized and thoroughly regulated, routine physical activity[12] for which the following features are characteristic:
- a competitive attitude, i.e., matching of strength, combativeness, and skill;
- the achievement of measurable and best possible results;
- economizing and rationalizing effort, with the aim of improving performance;

- discovering new ways and possibilities for achieving better results;
- general improvement of the physical form in regard to skillfulness, speed, strength, and stamina;
- preservation and improvement of personal health;
- strengthening of positive personal traits, self-confidence, and emotional stability.[13]

Because of its origin in the warring arts of the Far East, karate is one of the combat skills, which in English are generally referred to as "Martial Arts". However, karate became popular and widely-spread around the world only after it was developed as a combat sport. Otherwise, considering its dangers, it could hardly be practiced in any other form. In war, where it is a matter of life or death, the manner of fighting is fundamentally different from that in the sports arena. Sports fighting has to be, by its nature, conducted in such a way that the physical and mental health as well as the personal integrity of participants are not jeopardized.

How karate asserts itself as a sport is shown by comparing three components of the sport: (1) sports ethics, (2) sports contest, and (3) sports training.

Sports Ethics in Karate

Each of the martial art forms, including karate, has its own special code of ethics and morals that binds it with generally accepted social values and norms. The practise of karate becomes more a sport the further it gets away from its original purpose as a war skill. The sporting characteristics of karate make it able to be practiced in a way that does not jeopardize the life, health, or personal integrity of the participants. This, then, can mean two things:

First of all, one can only learn to be able to inflict physical injury – which is basically the aim of fighting – providing one realizes and fully understands, that human life and the personal integrity of each individual represent the highest social values. Personal respect and the protection of one's opponent from injury must be the elementary norm to be internalized by anyone learning karate. "Playful aggressiveness", which makes the requisite intuitive and unemotional fighting capability possible[14] must be accompanied by an absolute consciousness of responsibility, and this represents, at the same time, a threshold, which must never be crossed.

Secondly, the process of preparing a person for fighting in karate sport must involve more than just physical training. Besides mastering the fighting skill, a sportsman or sportswoman must also assimilate the proper codes of behavior used in the sporting bout as well as in everyday life. In addition to general "fair play", without which sports combat is hardly possible, a person must also develop all those spiritual, intellectual, emotional, and behavioral virtues, which are essential for his/her social integration particularly because a karate sportsman or sportswoman possesses a dangerous physical skill. For that reason he/she must always demonstrate, to a much higher degree than an average person, the presence and strength of his/her positive personal traits.

The Sports Contest in Karate

In the narrower sense, any sport is a competitive activity.[15] Competition is a form of testing one's physical and mental capability. An athlete tries, through endeavor, sacrifice and self control, to overcome the limits of the possible and thus surpass him or herself. His/her sporting achievements, manifested in victories and records, trace the progress being made and belong to cultural values.[16]

The testing of athletic ability is of course not possible without rules which (a) are equally valid for all participants and (b) define the conditions and manner of competing, as well as the manner in which results are measured. The rules of competition and therefore the rules of sports fighting in karate are actually an agreement amongst those wishing to compare their fighting capabilities with each other. This agreement lays down the circumstances under which the sports combat takes place, the permitted actions, penalized actions, methods of measuring the effectiveness of individual actions, as well as the general behavior of all participants.

The competition rules thus determine the degree of sportsmanship achievable in martial arts. They make a comparison of fighting abilities possible which is also in harmony with prevailing sports ethics as well as with the prevailing legal structure. Only in this way does sports combat attain its social legitimacy. The competition rules determine the degree of risk, by optimizing the balance between: (a) the stimulus to fight, and (b) the requirement to protect the health of the fighters i.e., between competitiveness and mutual respect.[17] The first one (a) depends on regulating favored actions, and on the criteria laid down for positive scoring. The second (b) depends on restricting the selection of actions and on the criteria for sanctioning them.

I believe that this is crucial in determining sportsmanship in the martial arts. Regulating the permitted and the restricted, i.e., by rewarding and penalizing, the competition rules provide the framework for the execution and development of the martial arts as a sport, giving direction for both its content and, in part, its methodology.

As in other combat sports, karate sports rules also demand the preference and selection of fighting techniques and tactics which are encouraged in the sporting bout.[18] The rules and regulations can, however, be neither rigid nor final. The rules offer a framework of limitations and guidelines only, within which different interpretations and variations are possible. They merely set a limiting framework, in which varying interpretations are possible, and these can be found in the individual repertoires as well as in the different methods of training, i.e., preparing for sports tournaments. Thus, it is quite normal (not only in karate) that within the currently valid competition rules, different schools, styles, and streams of karate exist side by side.

It is to be expected, that the functionality of the rules and regulations, particularly for instances where unexpected circumstances crop up in bouts, will continually be put to the test by individual innovative karate fighters, independent of the style to which they belong. Due to larger or smaller modifications to their individual fighting repertoire, and following their desire for success, they will occasionally use or create some fighting details which current competition rules do not regulate sufficiently. From time to time, when such deficiencies are discovered and accumulate, and even begin to annoy most of the participants, then the rules are renewed in accordance with practical needs. In this way the level of sportiness and sportsmanship in karate gradually rises.

Early forms of European karate-like fighting

A drawing from Thalhoffer's book on fighting. It was written in 1467, which makes it the oldest known book of its kind. Here, the defender is countering with a thrust front kick.

Sports Training in Karate

The sports competition-oriented practice of karate presupposes the existence of two things: (a) a fighting system, and (b) a teaching system.

The fighting system (a) is that repertoire or palette of fighting techniques and tactics which are selected, by virtue of the interpretation (and possibly future expected developments) of the current rules and regulations for sports tournaments. Each karate style or stream looks at sports fighting in its own unique way. But with regard to the selection of the sports fighting repertoire, each style must eventually comply with valid competition rules.

The teaching system (b) refers, in the wider sense, to the subdivision of selected fighting activities according to accepted methodical degrees of difficulty. This is usually called the *system of belts*. In the narrower sense, however, the teaching system refers to the methods of training at each particular level. Individual grades of one karate school can be very different from corresponding learning grades in another karate school. The grades can vary in their learning goals, extent, duration, process of training, and so on. Consequently, belts of the same level but from different schools can be weighted differently.

The picture in karate becomes blurred because, in addition to a repertoire of sports fighting actions, karate schools usually also teach other karate activities. The meaning, extent, and selection of these other activities can vary from style to style. Here we have the following in mind:
- a focus on the traditional requirements and aesthetics resulting in the cultivation of katas;
- a focus on strength training e.g., breaking bricks, boards etc;
- a focus on self-defense training e.g., different grips, holds, freeings, levers, and special strikes and kicks;
- a focus on hard-combat using various tools and weapons such as sticks (bo), chains, nunchakus, samurai swords, lances, and so on;

These additional activities are usually mixed into the training for a sports fighting repertoire. This has the effect of working against the requirement to optimize the time taken on training (i.e., increase the intensity) for sports tournaments.

The pervasive endeavor in sport to work towards the improvement and shortening of the preparation time for tournaments, demands always an economy and optimization of effort. This is one of the main characteristics of sports training. The

23

degree of sports-orientation inherent in particular karate schools is reflected in the degree of systematic and planned preparation of its members for sports fighting.

This demands:
a) the use of the most appropriate measures for the selection and priority of fighting techniques and tactics; this means making a clear distinction between sports activities and other activities in karate, and
b) in addition to the methodical classification of fighting activities, there should also be a phased and well conceived system of motivation and testing, the rapid integration of tournament experience, openness to new scientific findings regarding human mental and physical abilities – and so on – so that a fundamental framework of sports values and norms is built up.

With regard to their sports fighting systems, individual karate styles differ mainly in how they link different fighting techniques and tactics with each other. The possibilities lie between two extremes:
a) a large number of basic techniques, which are practiced as stereotypes in a small number of tactical situations, and
b) a small number of basic techniques, which are then practiced in a wide range of tactical variations.

In the teaching system, we observe the same differences: at each learning level, different karate styles give differing emphasis to chosen techniques or tactics.

In the same way as individual fighting systems are not bound to a certain form forever, teaching systems in particular karate styles are not unchangeable either. Both kinds of systems incorporate ongoing, spontaneous adaptation and rationalization, depending on practical experience in tournaments and observations made in training. In the future, sports science will play a greater role to this end. There are high expectations for further kinesiological research on the patterns of movement in karate, which will enrich kinesiology itself as well as trigger inevitable further shifts in the methods of training in karate sport.

FEATURES OF SPORTS COMBAT

The criteria by which we define the selection and priority arrangement of techniques and tactics, and the mutual linking of the two into a system of sports fighting actions, are acquired from two sources: from experience in sports tournaments and from training.

Sports combat is determined by use of the current competition rules and by a general understanding and interpretation of these rules. On the other hand, the sporting adequacy of a particular fighting system is reflected in (a) the way it considers and exploits the possibilities framed within the competition rules and their interpretations, and (b) how far it anticipates probable changes of the rules, thus opening further possibilities.

In the training process there is generally a noticeably high aspiration towards its intensification; one attempts to learn as much as possible in the shortest time possible. To that end, it is crucial that the contents of the training process are as easy to understand as possible. The more systematic and logical the content, the easier and faster the learning.

In the following pages, we will cover, firstly the characteristics of karate sports combat and the consequence of the use of fighting techniques and tactics. After that, we will run through the principles and elements of a structured schooling for karate sports combat. These illustrate the demands presented in putting together the requirements to be considered in the composition of the training – i.e., in the selected repertoire of fighting techniques and tactics. In conclusion we will summarize all the criteria considered in the fighting system for karate sports combat presented in this book.

The Characteristics of Karate Sports Combat

Karate sports combat is a competition in which each of the two participants demonstrate how they have been able to perfect the fighting techniques and tactics of the sport. Its function is to reveal which of the two opponents is better prepared for sports fighting. In a bout, each of the two fighters tries to achieve the same goal: to hit the opponent's vital points while at the same time protect his/her own vital points and prevent the opponent from hitting them. One is trying to maneuver his/her opponent into a vulnerable position where the opponent can neither protect his/her vital points nor escape or counter-attack. When the attacker is simultaneously in a favorable situation and at a suitable distance for an attack, and is ready to start it, we call this situation a *Tactical Moment*, (abbreviation – *TM*). Each of the two fighters tries to influence the course of the bout in such a way that as many as possible TMs occur for him/her, and as few TMs as possible for the opponent. (Further on this see p. 79 et seq)

Naturally, in the course of a karate sports bout a whole range of circumstances will occur which enable a comparison and assessment of proficiency to be made. As we will see, each circumstance will have a different consequence dependent on the selection of the fighting repertoire.

Duel

Sports combat in the martial arts, such as karate, is always a duel. Consequently, a fighter is preparing him-/herself for sports combat differently than he/she would do for self-defense, where a duel is only one of the many possible situations. Thus, for example, the starting position or "guard" in karate sport is adjusted to fighting with a single opponent, as it is in other similar types of combat sports, e.g., fencing or boxing. All fighting actions occur along one fighting axis which is a mobile one. One is able to concentrate exclusively on the position and actions of the opponent, and, accordingly prepare one's own strategy for the attack, without having to guard against unexpected attacks from other directions. Therefore all the maneuvering actions in the bout area are made with this specifically in mind.

Limited Bout Time

In sports combat, it has become a general rule that the actual fighting time is limited to two, and exceptionally three minutes. The time limitation constitutes the main considerable difference between karate as a martial art and karate as a combat sport.

Whereas karate as a martial art is practiced essentially for self-defense, (leaving aside for the moment its spiritual dimension), karate as a sport is – by its nature – offensive. Nevertheless, the traditional karate schools maintain that karate has a purely defensive character – despite the fact that their followers engage in karate sports combat. But let us think about this logically and consistently. Just imagine that in a sports bout the opponents only take defensive actions, each waiting for an attack from the other. In such a situation there would be no attack and consequently no combat, leaving no means to test the fighting skills – which is the purpose of sports combat. This kind of test is only possible if the opponents engage actively. Therefore at least one of them must attack at least once.

The limit on time in the sports bout spurs both opponents into activity, that is to attack, or at least into actively challenging. The purpose of this is to goad the opponent into an attack. Such behavior certainly could not be counted as defensive. Defense in karate sports combat is limited to the recovery of the situation in which one of the fighters, being too slow to launch an attack him-/herself, has been attacked by the opponent and has to prevent being actually hit him-/herself, and then counter-attack. Alternatively, perhaps one is in such an inferior position that he/she can only try to minimize the success of the opponents attack. However, the purpose of sports combat is not to test which of the two fighters is capable of more successfully defending him-/herself from an attack merely to prevent defeat, but rather to decide who is capable of quickly and convincingly winning. This is, however, only possible if one is active in directly attacking or if one incites the opponent to attack, thus creating the opportunity for a counter-attack. In a very real sense, a sports combat consists of attacks, counter-attacks, and counter-counter-attacks, etc. The time limit in a sports bout stimulates, directly or indirectly, offensive behavior and prevents the situation where both participants would perhaps even evade fighting and/or just wait for the right opportunity forever. Offensive conduct is characteristic in all combat sports, which of course influences the applied fighting repertoire, that is, the selection and priority of fighting techniques and tactics. Attack as a strategic basis of sports fighting definitely influences the compilation of fighting combinations presented in this book.

Limited Bout Area

The bout area in karate is usually flat and about eight meters square. Stepping across the line is penalized either with a warning or a point being awarded to the opponent. The latter consequence is the most logical because if one of the fighters has either intentionally or unintentionally left the arena, this is the same as capitulation, at least with regard to his/her strategic position in that moment of time. Limited space, therefore, has an effect similar to that of limited time: it spurs fighters into offensive conduct. Both of the fighters are thus motivated to fight actively by attacking the opponent. In this way, one will less probably be pushed out of the bout area, while the opponent, in turn, in trying to evade an attack, might step across the line.

Limited Number of Target Points

To prevent both participants from injuring each other, in sports karate it is not permitted to attack all the vital points of the human body. It is only permitted to

27

target the head and the upper body, above the belt. Attacks directed at the limbs, that is hands, arms and legs, do not count, while attacks against the protected points, such as the eyes, genitals, knees, shin-bone, etc., are penalized. This restriction also influences the selection of the fighting repertoire. It is indeed obvious that the technique, for instance, of a straight thrust kick looks different if it is directed towards the knee or genitals rather than the stomach.

Limited Selection of Impact Parts

Due to the obvious danger of injuries, it is forbidden to attack with the pointed or rather difficult to control extremities of the limbs such as pointed stretched fingers or the point of the elbow or knee. However, the latter restriction refers only to attacks toward the head or thrusts toward the spine, whereas strikes with elbows and kicks with knees to the body are acceptable, even though rarely used. In sports fighting, the fist is the most reliable weapon and is also most often used as the impact part for punches. Sometimes the edge or the heel of an open hand are also used. With kicks, all sides of the foot are used for impacts: the ball, outer-edge, heel, and instep, as well as the sole of the foot (sweeping). All of this is reflected in the selection of the fighting actions.

Controlled Hitting

To be considered valid, attacks on vital points have to comply with the restriction regulating the strength of the actual impact on hitting. The head, throat, and spinal cord are not allowed to be actually hit: any attack to these vital areas must stop just short of the target point, a light touch (touch control) being usually still tolerated. To the body, however, a light impact (impact control) is allowed. Contravention of this restriction is penalized with penalty points or even with disqualification.

Here we touch on one of the fundamental problems of sports combat in karate. The proper use of a genuine, full-scale karate punch or kick in a real fight would cause an injury to the opponent, and that is precisely what must not happen in a sports bout. In other combat sports, such as judo or boxing, the opponents are actually fighting each other and the consequences are obvious to everybody. In sports karate, however, the fight cannot be quite real, because the consequences would be fatal. Thus, in karate sports fighting, we encounter an almost unresolvable paradox: one has to pretend to do that which one is not really supposed to do, and if one actually does it, one will be penalized.

The requirement for full control of one's own punches and kicks also affects the technical execution of any particular attack. In an ideal situation, we must have complete control of the whole sequence of moves that constitute a particular attack, so that we shall be able to stop it at the very moment we actually could hurt our opponent. The effect of the impact, therefore, is measured in its potentiality. This means that the result of the actual fight is not quite realistic, while the actions are indeed real. An attack using controlled striking and without really hitting still has to be evaluated with regard to its effectiveness. Without this evaluation the sports bout would be meaningless. Since there must be no evident consequences of an attack to measure its effect – and indeed there must not be any – the recognition of the appearance of an attack is used to measure its effect and is therefore essential in estimating its potential power.

Importance of the Appearance of an Attack

A particular attack can be evaluated as successful if it simultaneously fulfills the following three conditions: (a) it occurs at the right moment, (b) it scores a controlled hit to the vital point, and (c) it is sufficiently powerful to have disabled the opponent if the hit had not been properly controlled.

The right moment and hitting the right spot can be judged by eyes alone and are obvious. However, the effectiveness of a hit can only be estimated indirectly by observing the sequence of actions and moves during the attack. Here we are talking about the transparency of the entire kinetic composition of an attack, from start to finish throughout all the intermediate transfers of acceleration from one part of the body to another. By observing the execution, an experienced referee can recognize whether the acceleration in individual phases of a particular attack is strong enough and if the movements consecutively accumulate in an optimum way, so that the attack concludes with a potentially effective hit. An ideal karate hit must be carried out in a synchronized activation of all the necessary muscle chains – in simple words, with the whole body – and this must be visibly recognizable by an observer. The better the execution, that is, the closer it is to the ideal – the "better" it looks, the "cleaner" the technique – the easier it is to evaluate it.

In sports combat, where positions are constantly changing, it is common that individual strikes will be executed often under unfavorable circumstances. Therefore, a particular technique may only be approximately "clean". The ability of referees to evaluate such techniques makes their job difficult. It makes sense, therefore, that the fighting repertoire should not consist only of individual strikes, but rather of a series of combined attacks called combinations. In this way a fighter can always continue with another attack if the previous attack has not been effective or if the referee has not counted it. Thus, it is extremely useful if a sports fighter is able to attack with combinations, and without interruptions in the flow of the motions. One has to be able to pass from one attack to the following one, with as

29

many hits in the sequence as are technically possible and tactically meaningful. One breaks off such a sequence of attacks, only if the fighter wants to, or if it comes to a halt spontaneously due to a change in the fighting situation, or if the referee stops the bout.

The use of combinations suits the spirit of active sports combat and simultaneously increases the possibility that at least one of the attacks will succeed and be recognized as successful by the referees. Additionally, if more than one attack in a series is effective, it is possible to gain more than one point in a single engagement. This possibility is also in harmony with the development of competition rules where a tendency toward a multi-point system is gradually becoming evident.

Restrictions with Repeated Attacks

In competitive practice we find that repeated attacks with the same hand are usually less effective and are also more difficult to recognize from their appearance. This happens when there is no repeated phase of bending (see p. 41 et seq) the hand between the first and second punch, that is, if the fighter does not take sufficient a swing before continuing with the next punch. The same applies to consecutive alternating punches, first with one hand and then with the other. Generally the latter kind of repeated punching is not considered by the referees. In the same way, repeated kicks, without an intermediate push-off from the floor, are considered only by exception.However, if one uses a series of attacks – foot-hand, foot-foot-hand or hand-foot-hand – in a flowing movement, the leading attack initiates the next. In this way every hit is performed through the activation of the whole body. Consequently, the potential effectivness of each individual attack does not come into question.

Limited Recognition of Techniques

According to prevailing competition rules, sports karate recognizes only punches, strikes and kicks, which of course target the vital points as described above. Other techniques which do not present clear karate attacks, even though they may temporarily disable the opponent, are not recognized. This includes sweeping, low throws (high ones are prohibited), blocks, deflection or any temporary barring of the opponent such as clinches. These techniques are only considered as preparatory actions for follow-up punches or kicks, and are as such indispensable in a sports fighting repertoire.

The Characteristics of Training for Sports Combat in Karate

Let us look now at the main requirements emanating from the process of sports training practice, which influence the selection of the sports fighting repertoire.

Sports Combat – The Point of Departure and the Training Objective

We have already mentioned that some traditional karate schools practise other fighting systems that do not belong to sports combat – i.e., katas, self-defense, breaking blows, the use of tools and weapons – and these have become mixed with the sports fighting system or have been even completely molded into it. Because of this, students of sports karate are obliged, at least to a certain degree, to master also other systems while learning the sports fighting system. This of course complicates the learning process and unnecessarily holds up the students in obtaining higher belts, thus delaying their entry into sports tournaments. Most of those other fighting systems have developed their own form of sports-orientation and even tournaments. Consequently they can be easily practised completely by themselves. This makes it possible to separate training for sports combat from those other types of exercises, and devote it exclusively to sports combat orientated techniques and tactics.

Logical Structure

We have already figured out that in sports combat, the correct and recognizable execution of attacks is necessary. The closer the execution of an attack to the ideal form (without taking into consideration any tactical conditions), the greater are its chances for a positive rating. Of course, perfection in performing a particular complex of motions implies relatively long and consistent training. This is a never-ending process whereby the ideal form is only gradually approached – though never finally reached – by continuously improving ourselves. This is the main reason that the learning process of sports karate is such a lengthy process, even though the learning content consists only of sports fighting techniques and tactics.

It is, consequently, obvious why the learning process as well as the subject of training must be as systematic as possible. The structure of the sports fighting repertoire plays a decisive role in this. The more it is systematized and made logical, the easier it is to organize a learning system which is shorter and more efficient for the training process. The requirement for logicality then means that all individual techniques and tactics must be compiled into an integral repertoire on the basis of their mutual relationships. The latter must then be visually and rationally

31

comprehensible and expressed through a suitable system of names and codes. The nomenclature of the sports fighting repertoire has to reflect the reciprocal interdependence of individual techniques and tactics.

Connection with the Theory of Human Kinetics.

One of the main conditions for an efficient economization of the training process in sports karate is the further reduction of extravagant and exotic elements, by replacing them with comprehensible, logical explanations of the movements in karate. It is becoming more and more obvious that karate has the same kinetic foundations as, and similar kinetic patterns to, many everyday activities and other sports. Insight of this kind has given us a solid basis for the systematization of the sports fighting repertoire, as well as a good orientation for empirical research in kinesiology.

Simplicity

Every learning process is arranged in a scale of levels or grades, according to the degree of difficulty of the subject to be learned. This is also the case in sports karate. Correspondingly, the sports fighting repertoire must be composed so that it can be easily subdivided into successive grades, according to degrees of difficulty. Our repertoire shall have, therefore, a relatively small number of basic elements. Based on comprehensible criteria, these basic elements will be logically divided into smaller units of applicable variation.

Flexibility

In the karate training process, as generally in every learning process, advanced students have a special role. It is expected from at least some of them, especially from the most experienced career contestants, that one or the other will have developed his/her own individual interpretation, as expressed in his/her fighting specialty which is in his/her individual variation of particular fighting actions. The sports fighting repertoire must contain flexibility for such openings or free areas without losing its character as a coherent logical system.

Capability of Development

The invention of new possibilities for the application of individual techniques and tactics happens in two ways; either (a) they are discovered in the training process and then tested in tournament practice, or (b) they stem from tournament experience and are analyzed and integrated into the sports fighting system and training process. The sports fighting repertoire must be composed in such a way that it allows for such adaptations, and eventually also for shifts in emphasis, without losing its character as a logical system. For this it must be a dynamic system.

The Characteristics of the Sports Fighting Repertoire

According to the requirements of sports fighting on the one hand, and of systematic training on the other, the sports fighting repertoire should have the following characteristics. It has to be:
- convenient for combat with one opponent;
- based on the attack as the principle strategy;
- composed of offensive actions, which
  - we can use in various combinations
  - flow from one to another without interruption
  - are mutually clearly discernible
  - can be properly controlled
  - can be continued also after finishing-off, if necessary;
- free from anything that is not directly used in sports combat;
- composed of comprehensively deducible kinetic elements;
- complete, systematic, and logical in its composition;
- composed of a small number of basic components, which, in their application, encompass a large number of variations;
- open for individual interpretation;
- adaptable and suitable for further development.

The fighting repertoire for sports karate combat presented here adheres to the above requirements, as closely as possible. In the following two major parts of the book, the first part deals with the technical and tactical basis of the sports fighting system, while the second part describes a pattern for their practical application in sports combat.

Two further scenes from ancient Greece. A part of the ancient Greek free-style fighting, called 'pankration' comprised the 'ortho-machia' – freely translated as 'standing-up fighting', in which most of the strikes, punches and kicks, known also in karate, were used. However, let us not forget that 'pankration' had been introduced already in the 33rd Olympic Games in 648 B.C. – i.e., hundreds of years before karate even developed.

The scene, in the top picture above, shows a deflection (scooping, Jap. – sukui-uke) and grasping of the attacking leg, while in the scene below, we see a punch with the left hand while the fighter is swinging with the right one for another punch. One can also see a referee (holding a stick) and on the vase in the bottom picture, there is a coach – just as it is nowadays in karate sports tournaments.

2. THE FIGHTING REPERTOIRE IN SPORTS KARATE

In everyday language, as well as in martial arts, there is no clear cut differentiation between the concepts of *technique* and *tactics*. This is understandable since in a fighting situation, a particular technique can only be used in one or the other tactical variation. On the other hand, each tactical variation always has its particular technical basis. However, this kind of differentiation is actually unimportant for the participants in a sports combat – contestants, referees and spectators alike. Their attention is concentrated on the effectiveness of individual actions, not on the differentiation between the technical and tactical elements of the actions.

Such a differentiation, however, becomes important in the process of learning sports fighting. The more comprehensible and consistent the differentiation between the technical and tactical elements of the fighting system is, the more the training process can be structured systematically.

By using the term *technique,* we mean the complex of movements that are necessary for the optimum execution of individual attacks in all three phases: initiation, execution, and conclusion. By optimum execution, we mean the best possible result, considering all psychomotor potentials of the performer in ideal tactical conditions. Ideal tactical conditions mean that the attacker does not need to consider any encumbrances; the opponent is presumed to be imaginary and is positioned in front of the attacker in a proper position and distance for the impending attack, without guarding him-/herself against the attack and no attempt at evasion is being made. Only under such ideal circumstances, without encumbrances of any kind, can the performer focus entirely on his/her own movements, so that we can speak of a "pure" (ideal, complete, or full-scale) technique.

Any disturbance or encumbrance influences the execution of each individual technique. In a sports bout, one's opponent is the main source of disturbances. He/she is moving back and forth, thus continuously changing the angles and distance from the attacker. Besides this, the opponent is also capable of attacking or responding with counter-attacks, which causes additional uncertainty for the attacker. Even if the opponent is not performing an attack or counter-attack, the pure possibility of this happening presents an uncertainty which sufficiently disturbs the attacker. Consequently, due to constant changes in the situation, the expectation of being actually hindered when attacking, and having to remove the opponent's protecting hands or prevent a counter-attack, the technique of the attacker can hardly be ideal. Additionally, other conditions can also be counted as disturbances; such as an unsuitable surface in the bout area, which can be too rough or too slippery, as well as the temperature of the air and floor, one's emotional state, and so on.

As soon as there are any disturbances or encumbrances during the execution of a technique – which in reality is, of course, the rule and not the exception – we have to apply tactics. In circumstances of actual or potential disturbances, encumbrances, or changes in the bout arena, the execution of any particular attack no longer depends on the capabilities of the performer only, but also on the conditions imposed. An originally pure technique has to be adapted to fit momentary situations in the bout arena and this means the application of appropriate tactical variations for certain techniques.

In the following passage first of all, the technical components of our fighting repertoire will be described. It begins with a comparison of the similarity of movements in other sports with those in karate. It shows those movements which we derive from other sports, and how they are linked into basic techniques and combinations for use in sports karate. This is followed by a review of the tactical components of karate fighting derived from the analysis of karate sports combat, concluding with a description of protective as well as active tactics.

TECHNICAL COMPONENTS

Similarities of Movements in Sports

In other sports it is possible to trace complex movements similar to those which we recognize in karate. Let us have a look at some examples (Figures 1–15):

Type of Sport:	Individual actions:	Karate actions:
fencing	attack with lunge	straight fist punch *(oi-tsuki)*
sprint	sprint start or running stride	reverse punch *(gyaku-tsuki)*
shot-put	putting the shot	reverse thrust with ball of hand *(gyaku-tsuki)*
handball	shooting at the goal from the hip-turn	reverse slap with edge or ball of hand *(gyaku-tetsui)*
hurdling	beginning of a jump	reverse front kick *(gyaku-mae-geri)*
football	volley kick	reverse round-house kick *(gyaku-mawashi-geri)*

We can discover even more amazing similarities in rhythmic gymnastics, figure skating, and even ballet. The similarities are not found only in individual actions, but in the complete structure of movements. Of course this should not surprise us, as the laws of human body movements are the same in all cases. The only variable is the use of particular movement chains for specific purposes in each particular sport. Hence, we can in karate, without reservation, apply kinesiology, particularly its morphological approach.

1	2	3	4

Figure 1–15:
Similarities of actions between karate and some other sports

5	6

7

Figure 1–9:
Similar movements in swinging and throwing

8	9

10   11

Figure 10–11: Similar course of a side jump kick

Figure 12–13: Similar start; at every stride we actually kick with the knee

12   13

Figure 14–15: Similar explosive lifting of leg during forward movement

15   14a   14b

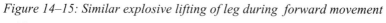

For our purposes, it is crucial to differentiate between cyclic (as in the sprint) and acyclic movements (as in the shot-put), especially with regard to the fact that each action consists of the three phases: initiation, execution, and conclusion.

Cyclic movement consists of alternating twisting motions (torsions, wringings) of the body from one side to the other with a simultaneous transfer of the body weight stepwise forward. At the end of each torsion and its accompanying step forward, we take up a reverse (diametrical, diagonal) body position. That is, we have two opposing parts of the body pushed forward: shoulder and arm of one side and the opposite leg. During the twisting of the body we experience a torsion of the torso, i.e., the shoulder (and arm) of the one side of the body moving in a direction opposite to the movement of the hips (and legs) of the same body side.

During each torsion of the body, we initiate a tension, which during its release in the sequence, supports the work of the starting leg in propelling the body forward into its next torsion in the opposite body position. One maintains his/her body balance by alternating the reverse positions. Cyclic movement is typical for walking and running. However, in some other sports, there are single cycles applied for various individual actions, for example, in most of the kicks in soccer. In a cyclic movement, the conclusion of the previous action melds with the initiation of the next action. Hence, there appear to be only two motion phases instead of three. Only the last of the cycles in the continuing cyclic movement comprises also a conclusion, thus consisting eventually of all three phases.

Intermittent acyclic movement is composed of elements such as twisting and untwisting of the body, translation of the whole mass of the body, leaning, ducking, and lifting of the upper body, turning of the head, etc. Twisting and untwisting of the body are two complementary movements that in most cases occur in alternating phases. In this way we usually have in one action – if we ignore other possible elements, which might serve the specific purpose of the action – either the sequence of untwisting-twisting-untwisting, or the sequence of twisting-untwisting-twisting. As examples of the first sequence are throws and thrusts specific for the shot-put, handball, and javelin throwing. The lunge in fencing could serve also as an approximate example of the second sequence.

Karate actions are composed of cyclic and acyclic (intermittent) movements. Our search for a dynamic pattern of movement which makes continuing attacks in uninterrupted series possible, suits the pattern of cyclic movement. From this all kinds of karate attacks, acyclic included, are derived.

The Sequence of Attacks in Karate

An explanation of the above can be made by observing the most commonly used attack in karate; a fist thrust or punch, that is, in the wider sense, a hand attack. We execute it mainly in two extreme forms. They differ from each other according to which leg is put forward in relation to the attacking hand. A hand attack can, hence, be executed:

- either as a counter-sided *(gyaku)*, diametrical, diagonal, or *reverse* hand attack, with the lead leg on the side opposite to the attacking hand,
- or as a same-sided *(oi)*, lead, one-sided, unilateral, or *straight* hand attack, with the lead leg on the same side as the attacking hand.

Attacks with legs, that is foot attacks, are performed also in the same two extreme forms.

Hand Attacks

a) Reverse attack

As an example of cyclic movement we take running or sprinting. A runner is moving forward with explosive strides (cf. figures 13, 14, p. 39). Let us look carefully at what is occurring during this motion. Each single stride happens in such a way that the body is moved forward by help of a push-off with the starting foot and a swing with the arm on the side of the body as the starting leg. This causes a sequence of the transfer of the body weight onto the standing foot. Simultaneously, the body is diametrically twisting and the standing foot becomes the starting foot. The next mirror cycle then begins. All the participating movements of the legs, arms, and trunk, which are being used for the creation, strengthening, and transfer of acceleration in such a cycle, are also used in reverse karate attacks.

For now, let us observe a hand attack. To make the execution of such an attack possible, the final acceleration with which we ideally hit the target must be at a maximum. Let us see what happens up to here. First we need a preparatory step. This causes the body to twist to the maximum extent, thus helping the arm to flex and prepare the hand for attack. This motion is similar to the bending[19] of an archer's bow. With the second step, all the accumulated energy is released, thus transferring the initial acceleration to the trunk twisting in the opposite direction and through it to the shoulder, extending arm, and attacking hand.

The biomechanics of the hand attack technique are as follows (see fig. 16–22, p. 46, 47):

◆ *First step:* Initiation of the attack:

Beginning in any stance, we take one step forward. With that, we push forward the shoulder, opposite to the lead leg, and extend the same arm – the palm thrown forward at shoulder height, while the edge of the hand is turned forward, and the elbow points downward. Meanwhile, we prepare the other arm for the attack by flexing it with a movement similar to punching backwards with the elbow, while forming simultaneously the same hand into a fist so that the thumb is turned towards the body, and holding it eventually in a ready position in front of the shoulder, next to our chest. Our step finishes in a reverse stance, in which our body weight is distributed so that there is slightly more weight on the front leg. Our body is upright and twisted to the uttermost, with the rear shoulder pulled back over the hips against the position of the heel, which remains anchored on the ground, while our hands are pulling away from each other, forward and backward, as if bending an invisible bow just before the release of the arrow (figure 26, p. 48). This stance – which is only visible for a fleeting moment since everything is moving quickly and our movements are uninterrupted – is loaded with a strong tension which facilitates the initiation of the next step, thus contributing to the acceleration of the actual hand attack. [20]

◆ *Second step:* Execution of the attack.

While executing the next step, we keep the hands as if they were bending a bow, until the forward moving leg becomes the lead leg, and we begin to set it down. However, the arms are not tensed while the shoulders as long as possible continue bending, thus keeping the accumulated tension of the body until the very last moment – when it is released all at once. The fist, staying in the ready position far from the actual target, has to hit it before the actual touch down of the front leg (which has now a rather short way to go) otherwise a part of the energy is lost into the ground. The right sequence of moving each particular body part, increases the whiplash effect thus maximizing the speed of the fist and with that the potential impact of the punch: body translation (sally or lunge), turning hips (twisting the body), releasing shoulders (untwisting), expanding the attacking shoulder (new twisting), and extending the attacking arm. The trajectory of the attacking fist approximates as far as possible a straight line. At the moment of the impact, the body is twisted ready for the next step. (Fig. 27, 28, p. 49).

b) Straight attack

In order to execute same-sided or unilateral, that is, straight attacks, we must slightly adjust both the aforementioned phases, i.e., the initial and the execution phase.

Let us first suppose that a preparatory step is performed in the same fashion as in a reverse attack (fig. 16–19, p. 46). After this the same-sided hand attack follows: the accumulated tension is released by an explosive turn (untwisting) of the body. The hands change their position sharply, one attacking, following the whip turn of the hips and shoulders, as in the first example, but this time we do not make the step forward. During a same-sided attack we actually suppress the step, which was necessary in the previously described reverse attack. Instead of this, the trailing leg pushes-off, the whole body is slightly forward, together with the lead leg. This is otherwise known as a lunge, or sally. When the attack is finished, we stand in a long straight stance or side stance, the body ready for the next twisting movement (fig. 20–21, p. 47). Everything else is, in principle, the same as in the reverse attack. The final maximum acceleration of the attacking hand or palm consists of various consecutive accelerations created by the translation of the body forward, unwinding of the hips followed by the shoulders, expanding of the attacking shoulder and the extending of the arm with the attacking hand.

With slight modifications, we can repeat this straight attack in a cyclic fashion, whereby we attack first with one hand and after that with the other side of the body and the corresponding hand.

Foot Attacks

The last phase of an attack with the hand is activated only during the leading foot's touch down and achieves its maximum acceleration at the moment just before or simultaneously as the foot lands on the floor. With this, we achieve a maximum transfer of acceleration into the targeted point, without losing any of it into the floor, which would happen if the foot landed too early. This is clearly visible if we draw the vector from the field of forces.

Contrary to this, the attack with the foot, or kick, is executed during our step. It maximizes the acceleration before the phase of the foot landing on the floor begins. Different attacks with the foot are attained with a variation of the attacking foot with the start, turning, extension of standing leg, and leaning of the torso. The work of the hands here is to keep the body balance necessary for the co-ordination of movement. There are different paths possible for the foot to travel, and these give us different kicks. We can systematize a great number of kicks used in sports fighting by creating six basic categories. We will present them in detail when we describe the combinations.

- Attack type I: step or lunge forward (fig. 33–35, 56–58, p. 55, 67);
- Attack type II: front thrust kick (*mae-geri*, fig. 38, 61, p. 57, 69);
- Attack type III: sweeping or hooking the opponent's leg
(*ashi-barai/ko-soto-bari*; fig. 41, 64, p. 59, 71);

- ◆ Attack type IV: front roundhouse kick
  (*mawashi-geri*, fig. 44, 67, p. 61, 73);
- ◆ Attack type V: back thrust kick after spin or half-turn
  (*ushiro-geri/ushiro-yoko-geri*; fig. 49, 73, p. 63, 75);
- ◆ Attack type VI: back roundhouse kick after spin or half-turn
  (*ushiro-mawashi/ura-mawashi-geri*; fig. 52, 76, p. 65, 77).

Each of the above mentioned types of attack has its reverse or straight version, depending on the position of the torso and hands. The two forms of each type of attack – reverse *(gyaku)* and straight *(oi)* – result in twelve basic kinds of foot attacks.

The Kinetic Scheme of Combined Attacks

Composition

Up to this point, we have been observing only the first two phases which can be repeated cyclically: preparation (initiation) and execution. However, when we want to finish-off any of the repeated cycles, or even the first execution, we get the three known phases of each full scale action: initiation, execution and conclusion. In the last cycle, the third phase is initiated in the same way as the first two phases – by a step and an explosive change in the positioning of the hands, while no further acceleration is added. Thus, this final move serves only as a finishing-off block, deflection, or barring. As this final action is applied just with the intention to stop moving forward, we suppress the final step. While turning the whole body in accordance with the changing of the position of the arms, the rear leg moves just a little closer to the lead leg, thus shortening the long attacking stance. In this way, we stand finally in the regular stance again, as at the beginning, ready for any new engagement. Therefore, we have two main options: after a reverse attack we stand in a same-sided, i.e., unilateral stance, while after a straight attack we stand in a diagonal, diametrical, or reverse stance.

In this way we get the basic three-phase scheme, which serves for a simple and smooth linking of hand-foot attacks into the basic combinations of two types: straight and reverse.

Firstly, we use our basic scheme for the technical performance of unilateral, straight combinations. As this is an analytical presentation, we begin from a reverse stance (which is, for clarity, not a fighting stance). We hold the hands in a transitional preparatory position, one close to the chest, while the other is partially extended, as if it had just executed a block-punch. After the step in the initial phase, we execute a straight hand attack in the second phase and complete it with a reverse block. Throughout the three phases, we actually make only one step forward, while the other two are suppressed. This sequence is presented in figures 16–22, p. 46, 47.

Next, we use our basic scheme for the technical execution of reverse combinations. For the sake of analytical presentation, it is best to begin in a unilateral stance. After the initial step, we attack in the second phase with another step and reverse open hand thrust. In the third phase, we perform a straight block as described above. Throughout the three phases, we perform two steps, while the third one is suppressed. This sequence is presented in figures 23–29, p. 48, 49.

Foot attacks are built into the three-phase system in the following way. In straight combinations, we attack with the foot in the first phase diagonally, that is reverse, and with the hand in the second phase unilaterally, that is straight. The foot and hand on the same side of the body perform the attack. In reverse combinations, we attack with the foot in the second phase unilaterally, that is straight, and in the same phase also with the opposite hand diagonally, that is reverse. In the backward kicks, however, this kind of differentiation is less indicative due to the full turning or halfway reverting, and will be therefore indicated in parentheses or omitted.

Before a more detailed description of the corresponding photographs is presented, the principles of nomenclature and coding used must be explained.

Naming and Coding

Meaningful naming and the selection of symbols or codes for the differentiation of individual stances, postures, actions, and combinations is crucial for a good understanding and quick comprehension of the fighting system. Using the naming scheme presented here, the mutual relationships of individual stances and actions become clear.

First, we must differentiate, by the use of symbols, the right and left hand from the right and left leg. This is presented in the following chart:

side	right	left
hand	A	B
leg	R	L

To fig. 16:
Initial position: Reverse stance (gyaku-dachi). The hands are stretched apart. The right one is in the forward position and turned so that the palm edge leads, while the left fist is in the preparatory position beside the chest, the shoulders are not yet flexed for attack, both elbows facing downwards; legs are slightly bent, the body weight is slightly more on the front foot, the pelvis slightly tilted upwards, while the shoulders are loose, and the head is upright.

To fig. 17:
Approximately one-third of the first phase. The start is initiated with an explosive extension of the rear leg, inducing a transfer of the body weight forward, there is a twisting (torsion) of the right hip and the whole right side of the torso as well as an extension of the right arm straight forward. Simultaneously, the left side of the body and the left hand are pulled back. In this way, the body twists and accumulates tension, which we can utilize in the next phase.

To fig. 18:
Approximately two-thirds of the first phase, which we can also utilize for various foot attacks. Here, the starting leg has reached the forward position shortly before touching down. The left, standing leg is in the meantime taking over the complete weight of the body; with a pushing-off motion and extension it is giving the body additional acceleration; the body has just been released from the previous torsion and has begun twisting in the opposite direction. The hands are starting to exchange positions.

To fig. 19:
End of the first phase: reverse stance (gyaku-dachi). The step with a preliminary block-punch and the preparatory bending (flexing) of the right shoulder and arm is complete. This is not a static stance: the body is twisted to the extreme, tending to release the accumulated tension into an attack, which follows.

To fig. 20:
Approximately one half of the second phase. In-
stead of using a second step, the tension is re-
leased solely through the unwinding of the torso,
that is, by extending the upper body: the complete
left side of the body (leg, hip, torso) twists away
from the direction of the attack, while the right
body side turns forward and the right hand is
explosively triggered into attack, and the left
hand begins to move in the opposite direction
towards the chest.

To fig. 21:
End of the second phase: side stance (oi-dachi).
Shortly before finishing the interchanging of
hands, which represents the main attack – there is
a direct thrust with the edge of the palm, or block-
punch (oi-shuto) – simultaneously drawing the
hand back for the next hit, the body has become
completely unwound. The back leg, turned away
from the attack, will now begin a new start with a
push of the left body side forward.

To fig. 22:
End of the third phase: Reverse stance (gyaku-
dachi). The twist of the left leg is explosively
transferred through the left hip onto the shoulder
and from there, its force is transmitted to the left
hand, (while it has still moved in the opposite
direction), thus launching the finishing-off block-
punch (gyaku-shuto). In the new reverse position,
the body is ready for a further three-phase cycle.

Figures 16–22:
The sequence of the three-phase scheme for STRAIGHT combinations

23

To fig. 23:
Initial position: side stance (oi-dachi). The hands are in the preliminary position, the legs are slightly bent, the feet are at shoulder width, one step apart, and turned so that they are in alignment with the position of the hips; the pelvis is slightly tilted upwards, shoulders loose and down; the back of the head is held high; body weight is slightly more on the front foot.

24

To fig. 24:
Approximately one-third of the first phase. Side start begins; this is a variation of the usual start. The body is accelerated forward entirely from a push-off with the rear leg and slight twist of the right hip. The shoulders and hands are not involved in this move.

25

To fig. 25:
Approximately two=thirds of the first phase. The starting leg moves forward and has reached the standing front leg, which has just taken over the full body weight and is beginning to give the forward-moving body additional acceleration. The torso, shoulders and hands are still not involved.

26

To fig. 26:
End of the first phase: reverse stance (gyaku-dachi). The introductory step is finished. The body is extremely twisted. The rear leg is initiating a new start. The shoulders and hands are still in the same position yet extremely flexed, each in the opposite direction.

27

To fig. 27:
Slightly more than half of the second phase. In this phase, various foot attacks can be executed: here, we are in the middle of a stride forward. The standing leg has already begun to deliver additional acceleration whilst pushing the body forward. The body has unwound itself, yet has already started to twist in the opposite direction.

28

To fig. 28:
End of the second phase: reverse stance (gyaku-dachi). Our step has been completed. Whilst the front foot touches down, the main attack has been performed with the right hand – in this instance, a reverse block-punch with the outer edge of the palm – while the left hand has been pulled back into a preparatory position beside the chest. The body is twisted again and is already beginning the push-off and unwinding of the right leg, thus inducing an attack with the left hand.

29

To fig. 29:
End of the third phase: side stance (oi-dachi). The step is suppressed, the right leg has stayed on the spot. The acceleration that extended the left hip forward has been transferred to the left shoulder and its force has been transmitted to the left hand, which has been launched into a finishing-off block, while the other hand has been pulled back into a preliminary position beside the chest. The momentum of the acceleration is now expended, the body has been unwound and is ready for another start.

Figures 23–29:
The sequence of the three-phase scheme for REVERSE combinations.

For the designation of the hands, we have used capital letters A (right) and B (left), while the capital letter R designates the right leg, and L the left one.

Furthermore, using symbols we designate also the same-sided, straight, or side stance (S) and the reverse, diagonal, or diametrical stance (D), alternating R, the right stance or L, the left stance, according to which leg is in the front position (the right or the left leg) at the time. If the feet are parallel and at a right angle to the opponent, which is a position we use in some elementary exercises but is in fighting practice a pure coincidence, we name it a neutral position.

stance	right (R)	left (L)
side (S)	RS	LS
reverse (D)	RD	LD

Attacks, or rather all actions with the hand, we designate according to whether they are performed with the right (A) or left (B) hand and in either a straight (1) or reverse (2) form.

attack with hand	right (A)	left (B)
straight (1)	A1	B1
reverse (2)	A2	B2

Foot attacks we designate firstly, according to the type, using Roman numerals I–VI, as already indicated above. Considering the execution and type we designate them with uneven numbers (1, 3, 5, 7, 9, 11) if they are reverse, or with even numbers (2, 4, 6, 8, 10, 12) if they are straight. The reason why will be understandable by viewing the table of all the combinations (table 1) based on this same principle. Reverse foot attacks actually introduce straight hand attacks on the same side, while straight foot attacks introduce reverse hand attacks with the hand of the opposite side.

attack with foot	right (R)	left (L)
reverse	(R1),R3,R5,R7,R9,R11 introducing A1	(L1),L3,L5,L7,L9,L11 introducing B1
straight	(R2),R4,R6,R8,R10,R12 introducing B2	(L2),L4,L6,L8,L10,L12 introducing A2

There is actually no practical need to code the foot attacks 1 and 2, because there can be confusion with the codes for hand attacks 1 and 2, which already include these two foot attacks. Instead we name them directly a step (foot attack 2) or a lunge, sally or slide forward (foot attack 1). They are not real attacks anyway, as they are neither directed against a vital point, nor disturb the opponent's balance. Instead, they really only "attack" the distance to the opponent. (This is why we have shown them in parentheses in the table above.)

The types of combinations we code as following: the straight ones with S and the reverse ones with D (diagonal, diametrical); or according to types of foot attack with I–VI. To distinguish individual combinations, we use combined shortened coding for attacks with the foot and hand. For example, for the combination of a reverse sweep of the opponent we use the code (R5), which is followed by a straight punch (A1). So it suffices to use the code 5A instead of a combined R5A1. At the beginning it seems confusing, but one gets easily used to it.

A little later in the book, in the tactical part, we will have to integrate two spatial concepts which we use for the description of fighting situations. These two terms are similar but not the same: *fighting axis* and *axis of attack*. The fighting axis is the line between each of the centers of balance of the two opponents. The axis of attack, however, is the line between the attacking foot or fist of the attacking fighter and the vital point of the defending opponent. A third spatial concept which we should explain at this juncture is called the *line of attack*. This is the trajectory, which is described by the foot or hand in the course of an attack. Other spatial concepts we will explain later in the tactical part of the book (see legend to fig.100, p. 94).

Competitors in a sports fight we name as either the attacker or the defender (opponent). In an actual sports fight, one wears a red belt and the other a white one. So we code them as Red or White, or even sometimes X and Y.

The Characteristics of Basic Combinations

The six types of attacks carried out in a straight or reverse form give a total of twelve basic combinations. These are technical stereotypes in our fighting repertoire. Table 1 gives us an overview of this framework, within which there is a multitude of practical applications possible. This overview shows how individual combinations are composed. In explanation of Table 1, we can summarize some of the characteristics of these basic combinations.

- ◆ A basic combination is an uninterrupted series of foot and hand attacks, which is completed with a finishing-off action.
- ◆ Basic combinations are built up according to a three-phase scheme for the attack with the hand: i.e., phases of initiation, execution and finishing-off.
- ◆ There are two forms of combinations:
  - • straight, in which the foot and hand of the same side are attacking, and are indicated using uneven numbers from 1 to 11.

Table 1: Review of basic combinations

COMBINATION

		1	2	3	4	5	6	7	8	9	10	11	12
Type		I		II		III		IV		V		VI	
Form	Straight (same sided)	S		S		S		S		S		S	
Form	Reverse (diagonal)		D		D		D		D		D		D
Number		1	2	3	4	5	6	7	8	9	10	11	12
Variation		A B	A B	A B	A B	A B	A B	A B	A B	A B	A B	A B	A B

FOOT ATTACK

		1	2	3	4	5	6	7	8	9	10	11	12
Direction		forward (front)								backward (back)			
Trajectory		thrust				roundhouse				thrust		roundhouse	
Kind		step/slide		kick		sweep		kick		kick		kick	
Type		I		II		III		IV		V		VI	
Number		1	2	3	4	5	6	7	8	9	10	11	12
Form	Straight (same sided)		S		S		S		S		S		S
Form	Reverse (diagonal)	D		D		D		D		D		D	
Side	Right	R	R	R	R	R	R	R	R	R	R	R	R
Side	Left	L	L	L	L	L	L	L	L	L	L	L	L

HAND ATTACK

		1	2	3	4	5	6	7	8	9	10	11	12
Direction		forward											
Trajectory		thrust											
Kind		punch											
Type		I											
Number		1	2	1	2	1	2	1	2	1	2	1	2
Form	Straight (same sided)	S		S		S		S		S		S	
Form	Reverse (diagonal)		D		D		D		D		D		D
Side	Right	A	A	A	A	A	A	A	A	A	A	A	A
Side	Left	B	B	B	B	B	B	B	B	B	B	B	B

- reverse, in which the foot and hand of opposite sides are attacking, and are indicated using even numbers from 2 to 12.
- Every attack with a foot introduces an attack with the hand, namely:
  - in straight combinations, reverse foot attacks in the first phase introduce straight hand attacks in the second phase;
  - in reverse combinations, straight foot attacks in the second phase introduce reverse hand attacks in the same phase.
- Concerning foot attacks there are:
  - six types of combinations, which we indicate in the same way as the foot attack types, namely with Roman numerals I to VI,
  - twelve kinds of combinations, which we indicate using the numbers from 1 to 12.
- Concerning hand attacks, there are two possible executions for each of the combinations:
  - execution A, when the right hand is attacking, and
  - execution B, when the left hand is attacking.
- Every combination is finished-off in the third phase with an explosive changing of hands, which serves to block or bar the opponent's hands and simultaneously to reinstate readiness for a possible new attack, as follows:
  - straight combinations end with a reverse finishing-off, and
  - reverse combinations end with a straight finishing-off action.
- If we begin all combinations in a side stance – throughout this book an assumption is made that the beginning is made from a left side stance – then we move while attacking:
  - with straight combinations altogether one step forward, and
  - with reverse combinations altogether two steps forward.

It is important to stress that the next chapter presents the basic combinations in their analytical form (i.e., not the tactical one): each single move is made in a pure and complete manner, and, to the maximum extent possible.[21] Also, they begin with a transitory stance (i.e., not in the fighting one):
- straight combinations with a reverse stance, and
- reverse combinations with a side stance.

All of the A-combinations laid out are analyzed and described in detail together with illustrated figures (photos). First, there are the straight and then the reverse combinations. The B-combinations are omitted because they are simply mirror images of the As.

Since foot and hand attacks vary in their range and can be executed at differing distances, and, in order to be able to carry out each of the combinations in their entirety, it has been presumed that the imaginary opponent has withdrawn to an ideal distance sufficiently, so that the follow-up fist attack can flow on from the initiating foot attack.

30	31	32
Reverse initial stance (gyaku-dachi)	*Start*	*Pushing-off and extension of support leg begins*

Straight Combinations

Combination 1A

Fig. 30:
Initial position: left transitory reverse stance LD (gyaku-dachi, see also fig. 16). The right side of the body (leg, hip, shoulder) is twisted and the right hand held forward, not quite extended, the left hand flexed, with the fist in a launching position beside the chest, not strained but ready to attack; the body weight leans slightly forward.

Fig. 31:
Approximately one-fifth of the first phase. The reverse start begins (see also fig. 17). The push-off and extension of the right leg leads to the right hip and shoulder turning as well as the right arm thrusting forward, while the left arm is flexed, the fist is beside the chest ready for a punch (visualize holding the arms approximately like bending an imaginary bow). The body weight has been explosively transferred forward, the right side leading and, consequently, the wringing of the body reaches its peak. The strain of the torsion is now at a maximum: when it is released it assists the actual start of the attacking leg.

Fig. 32:
About half of the first phase. The tension has been released by the start of the attacking right leg and unwinding of the body, which is now twisting to adopt the opposite wringing. The right leg is now beside the left support leg which has taken over the whole body weight and is just beginning to transfer it back onto the right leg moving forward; simultaneously, the upper part of the body is switching the leading side and the hands are just changing positions.

Fig. 33:
About four-fifths of the first phase. The right leg, being now already in the front position, is being accelerated further as a result of the push-off and extension of the support left leg, which is also causing further torsion of the left hip and shoulder in the opposite direction and, consequently, a bending of arms.

54

Please, cut out this part along the indicated line and the edge of the photograph in order to obtain the correct overview of the combination.

33	34	35	36
In the mid-step	Bending for punch	Straight punch with the fist (oi-tsuki)	Finishing-off: reverse block punch (gyaku-shuto)

Fig. 34:
End of the first phase: dynamic right reverse bending posture. The right foot is still in the air, just about to land, while the hands are bending for a punch. The support leg is still propelling the body forward, whilst the body is completely wrenched and thus strained to the maximum. The release of the accumulated tension begins with the right hip beginning to move forward, which in turn "cuts" the backward-moving right shoulder with the flexed right hand, thus eventually effecting an amplified, whiplike launching of the right hand fist punch.[20]

Fig. 35:
End of the second phase: Regarding appearance and power, this is the climax of the hand attack, that is, of the straight right fist punch to the head (oi-tsuki-jodan); at this very moment, the whole chain of muscles which effect the punch have to be contracted in order to intercept and compensate for the backlash of the impact (here only imaginary). The final acceleration that has culminated in the punch, emanates from: (a) the further rotation, i.e., unwinding the body, (b) the translation i.e., further moving forward of the whole body – between the launching of the fist and the impact – and (c) the expansion of the shoulder forward, and finally, (d) the extension of the arm. At the moment of impact, the movement of the body forward has not yet finished as the foot is still in the air. The excessive extension of the body, the extremely long attacking stance as well as the strained muscles at the very moment of the impact result in a new tension – which is released in the finishing-off action which follows.

Fig. 36:
End of the third phase: final position – right transitory reverse stance RD (gyaku-dachi). The final tension has been released by a light start of the left foot and a short movement forward of the whole body, as well as by the twisting of the left hip forward followed by the twisting of the shoulders and an explosive change of hands with a finishing-off reverse block-punch. The left leg has moved closer to the front leg, thus shortening the long attack stance into a final stance, which is about the same length, and of the same form, as the initial stance. With this, combination 1A is completed. We are ready for a new start.

Please, cut out this part along the indicated line and the edge of the photograph in order to obtain the correct overview of the combination.

30
Reverse
initial stance
(gyaku-dachi)

31
Start

37
Launching of front
reverse thrust kick

Combination 3A

Fig. 30:
Initial position: left transitory reverse stance LD (gyaku-dachi).

Fig. 31:
Approximately one-fifth of the first phase. Beginning of the start.

Fig. 37:
Approximately one-half of the first phase. After the start with the right leg, the right knee has been lifted up to the height of hips, the leg is flexed in order to perform a knee kick toward the stomach area. This is the chambering or launching position in which the leg is just passing, and as a result is receiving additional acceleration from the push-off and extension of the left support leg. Following the twisting of the shoulders, the left hand has just begun to take over the lead of the foot attack by a thrust kick to follow.

Please, cut out this part along the indicated line and the edge of the photograph in order to obtain the correct overview of the combination.

✂

38	39	35	36
Front reverse thrust kick (gyaku-mae-geri)	Rechambering, bending for the punch	Straight punch with the fist (oi-tsuki)	Finishing-off: reverse block punch (gyaku-shuto)

Fig. 38:
About four-fifths of the first phase. Regarding form and power, this is the climax of the front reverse thrust kick (gyaku-mae-geri) with the right foot to the body. The final acceleration, which is transferred to the target (here only imaginary), emanates from movement of the whole body forward – the hips being pushed forward by the support leg – and a snapping extension of the kicking leg. At the moment of impact (here imaginary) there is a contraction of the complete chain of the muscles involved, together with the stomach muscles, from the support into the attacking leg, the hips and stomach muscles being the mediators between the two. The body and arms, keeping the torsion, serve solely to provide proper co-ordination and balance, and are preparing the follow up hand attack.

Fig. 39
End of the first phase: dynamic right transitory posture. After the impact, the lower part of the kicking leg has been explosively and completely pulled back into the chambering position. Whilst preparing for the foot landing, the body has been completely wrung and the shoulders and arms are bending for the fist punch.

Fig. 35:
End of the second phase: right straight hand punch (oi-tsuki).

Fig. 36:
End of the third phase: final position right transitory reverse stance RD (gyaku-dachi). With this combination 3A is completed. We are ready for a new start.

Please, cut out this part along
the indicated line and the
edge of the photograph in
order to obtain the correct
overview of the combination.

30	31	40
Reverse	*Start*	*Launching of*
initial stance		*the sweep*
(gyaku-dachi)		

Combination 5A

Fig. 30:
Initial position: left transitory reverse stance LD (gyaku-dachi).

Fig. 31:
Approximately one-fifth of phase one. The start with the right leg has just begun.

Fig. 40:
Approximately one-half of phase one. The right, attacking leg has begun to move forward,
describing a half circle just above the ground and is passing its launching position parallel
to the left support leg. The left leg, taking over the whole of the body weight, is beginning
to support the forward moving right leg by pushing the hips forward. Simultaneously, the
upper body is beginning to lean backwards while the shoulders are twisting reversely and
the left arm is taking over the lead.

Please, cut out this part along the indicated line and the edge of the photograph in order to obtain the correct overview of the combination.

41	42	35	36
Reverse sweeping (ashi-barai)	Rechambering and bending for the fist punch	Straight punch with the fist (oi-tsuki)	Finishing-off: reverse block punch (gyaku-shuto)

Fig. 41:
Approximately four-fifths of phase one. This is the climax of the reverse sweeping (ashi-barai) of the front leg of an imaginary opponent. The attacking leg has moved explosively in a semi-circle from right to left and also slightly forward, the foot is turned in order to hit the lowest part of the opponent's leg with the flat of the sole. The final acceleration of the sweeping foot emanates, in this attack, from the forward-pushed hips. With the strong wringing of the shoulders, diametrical to the sweeping movement, and backward leaning position of the body (in the figure, this phase of leaning backwards is not visible any more, as it has already occurred) we maintain a proper and dynamic balance while attacking.

Fig. 42:
End of phase one: dynamic right reverse transitory posture. The strong wringing of the body makes it possible to stop the swing of sweeping and enables one to pull the attacking leg back along the axis of attack again. The bending of the shoulders and arms is completed, and using the forward driving right hip, the fist punch will be launched.

Fig. 35:
End of the second phase: right straight fist punch (oi-tsuki).

Fig. 36:
End of the third phase: final position – right transitory reverse stance RD (gyaku-dachi), with a left hand finishing-off block-punch. Combination 5A is thus completed and we are again ready for a new start.

Please, cut out this part along the indicated line and the edge of the photograph in order to obtain the correct overview of the combination.

30	31	43
Reverse initial stance (gyaku-dachi)	*Start*	*Chambering for front roundhouse kick*

Combination 7A

Fig. 30:
Initial position: left transitory reverse stance LD (gyaku-dachi).

Fig. 31:
Approximately one-fifth of phase one. The start of the attack with the right leg has just begun.

Fig. 43:
Approximately one-half of phase one. The right, attacking leg has been flung out – flexed and with the knee leading – into a chambering or launching position for a roundhouse kick. To this purpose, the upper body has begun a reverse twist, the arms are changing their positions, and the body is inclining slightly to the side. The support leg has taken over the complete body weight, and has begun to add additional acceleration to the right leg by pushing-off, extending, as well as by turning and driving the right hip forward. A launching of the lower right leg into a roundhouse kick will follow eventually, with further simultaneous wringing and inclining of the body.

Please, cut out this part along the indicated line and the edge of the photograph in order to obtain the correct overview of the combination.

44	45	35	36
Front reverse roundhouse kick (gyaku-mawashi-geri)	Rechambering and bending	Straight punch with the fist (oi-tsuki)	Finishing-off: reverse block punch (gyaku-shuto)

Fig. 44:
Approximately four-fifths of phase one. This is the climax of the front reverse roundhouse kick (gyaku-mawashi-geri) to the head. The final acceleration emanates from the combined effect of previous accelerations, which arose from the actions of the support leg (push-off-extension-rotation), the twisting of the hips, as well as from the work of the attacking leg muscles when lifting the thigh and snapping the lower leg in a semi-circle to the targeted point. Inclining the torso, twisting the body and bending of the shoulders and arms serve to maintain the dynamic body balance for the hand attack to follow.

Fig. 45:
End of phase one: a dynamic right reverse transitory posture. After the attack, the snapping back of the lower leg and rechambering assist the straightening up of the upper body, whereby the shoulders are twisted and the arms are bending as much as possible in order to launch the fist punch. The right hip has just begun to move forward, thus initiating the launching of the fist punch to follow.

Fig. 35:
End of the second phase: right straight fist punch (oi-tsuki).

Fig. 36:
End of the third phase: final position – right transitory reverse stance RD (gyaku-dachi) is established. With this, combination 7A is completed, and we are ready for new start.

61

Please, cut out this part along the indicated line and the edge of the photograph in order to obtain the correct overview of the combination.

30	46	47	48
Reverse initial stance (gyaku-dachi)	*Cross-step*	*Turning of the body*	*Chambering for the back (reverse) thrust kick*

Combination 9A

Fig. 30:
Initial position: left transitory reverse stance LD (gyaku-dachi).

Fig. 46:
About one-tenth of phase one. The left foot moves across the right foot axis of attack, thus beginning a rotation of the body.

Fig. 47:
Approximately one-third of phase one. After turning 180 degrees on the ball of the left foot, the position of the arms changes, and the head has turned as well and is now looking over the right shoulder. (Alternatively , there should be no change of arms, and the head remains turned over the left shoulder). We stand in a left backward reverse stance, ready for a backwards start.

Fig. 48:
Approximately one-half of phase one. After the start, the right leg has been chambered into the launching position for the back reverse thrust kick

Please, cut out this part along the indicated line and the edge of the photograph in order to obtain the correct overview of the combination.

49	50	35	36
Back (reverse) thrust kick (ushiro-geri)	*Continuation of turning with rechambering and bending*	*Straight punch with the fist (oi-tsuki)*	*Finishing-off: reverse block punch (gyaku-shuto)*

Fig. 49:
About two-thirds of phase one. This is the climax of the back (reverse) thrust kick (ushiro-geri) to the body. We have explosively catapulted the striking leg along the axis of attack, the heel of the attacking foot hereby dragging forward after being first lifted up to the target height. The final acceleration in play here, emanates from an intensive inclination of the upper body and from the explosive extension of the kicking leg. The position of arms and head remain unchanged.

Fig. 50:
About four-fifths of phase one. Rechambering by a flexion of the right leg with a simultaneous twist of the thigh upwards, the left shoulder and arm lead further turning the whole body in the direction of the attack – beginning with a turn on the heel of the support leg – and then straightening up the upper part of the body. The final phase of the bending for the fist punch follows.

Fig. 35:
End of the second phase: right straight fist punch (oi-tsuki).

Fig. 36:
End of third phase: final position – the right transitory reverse stance RD (gyaku-dachi) is established. Combination 9A is thus finished, and we are ready for the next start

Please, cut out this part along
the indicated line and the
edge of the photograph in
order to obtain the correct
overview of the combination.

30	46	47	51
Reverse initial stance (gyaku-dachi)	*Cross-step*	*Turning of the body*	*Launching the back (reverse) roundhouse kick*

Combination 11A

Fig. 30:
Initial position: left transitory reverse stance LD (gyaku-dachi).

Fig. 46:
About one-tenth of phase one. Cross-stepping over the right foot's axis of attack in preparation for a rotation.

Fig. 47:
Approximately one-third of phase one. The whole body has turned 180 degrees, the arms therefore changing their positions and the head turning to look over the right shoulder. The backwards start for a roundhouse kick is just beginning.

Fig. 51:
About one-half of phase one. We have pushed-off with the right attacking leg slightly angled upward and away from the support leg. The attacking leg has just passed the launching position. It has gained additional momentum through the inclination of the torso, and from the work of the leg muscles during the whole spin with the semi-extended leg.

52	50	35	36
Back (reverse) roundhouse kick (ushiro-mawashi-geri)	Continuation of the spin with rechambering and bending	Straight punch with the fist (oi-tsuki)	Finishing-off: reverse block punch (gyaku-shuto)

Fig. 52:
About two-thirds of phase one. The climax of the back (reverse) roundhouse kick (ushiro-mawashi-geri) to the head. The final acceleration of the kick emanates from the inclination of the upper body and from the work of the muscles when lifting and snapping back the attacking leg. While the position of arms and head remain unchanged, the upper body has, besides leaning forward, also jerked slightly in the direction opposite to the attack in order to compensate for the inertia of the hit.

Fig. 50:
Approximately four-fifths of phase one. The lower part of the attacking leg has snapped along the last part of the attacking path, away from the target, then rechambered with the thigh turned upwards, while the whole body has been turned further in the direction of the attack and the upper body straightened up. It follows the bending for the fist punch.

Fig. 35:
End of the second phase: right straight fist punch (oi-tsuki).

Fig. 36:
End of the third phase: final position – the right transitory reverse stance RD (gyaku-dachi) is established. Combination 11A is thus completed and we are ready for the next start.

65

53	54	55
Initial	*Preliminary*	*Set-up for the*
side stance	*step*	*attacking step*
(oi-dachi)		

Reverse Combinations

Combination 2A

Fig. 53:
Initial position: left transitory side-stance LS (oi-dachi). The hands are in a transitory side position (compare fig. 23), the left hand is in front, while the right arm is flexed, the fist is held beside the right chest in the launching position. A straight start (compare figs. 24, 25) for the preliminary step is beginning.

Fig. 54:
End of the first phase: right transitory reverse stance (compare fig. 26). The preliminary step is completed. Now the body is wrung and the forward driven left shoulder and hip are introducing the start of the left attacking leg (compare fig. 31).

Fig. 55:
Approximately one-third of phase two. The position of the arms remaining unchanged, the body and the left leg keep moving forward. The right leg has just taken over the full body weight and is beginning to deliver additional acceleration to the forward movement of the body.

66

Please, cut out this part along the indicated line and the edge of the photo in order to obtain the correct overview of the combination

56	57	58	59
In the middle of the attacking step	Bending for the fist punch	Reverse fist punch (gyaku-tsuki)	Finishing-off: straight block (oi-shuto)

Fig. 56:
About two-thirds of phase two. The continuing movement of the left body side and the attacking leg forward has been unwinding the body.

Fig. 57:
Approximately four-fifths of phase two. The left foot is about to land, the torso is completely unwound along the axis of attack, shoulders and hands are bending, ready for the fist punch. The right heel has just turned outwards, causing a tension in the body, and which will be released by a whiplash-like chain of motions launching the fist attack.[20]

Fig. 58:
End of the second phase. This is the climax of the right reverse fist punch to the body (gyaku-tsuki-chudan), which happens just prior to, or at the latest, simultaneously to the touchdown of the leading foot. The final acceleration emanates from a synergy of the whipping motion of the right body side subsequently driving the right hip and shoulder further forwards, the extension of the attacking arm, and the inertia of the body moving forward before the touchdown of the foot. At the moment of impact (here imaginary) the chain of body and arm muscles co-operating in the punch become strained for a moment. In this way, we prevent a possible distortion of the hand, arm or body position that could result from a backstrike of the target. The new tension accumulated, as a result of wringing during the punch, is released by the finishing-off action to follow.

Fig. 59:
End of the phase three. Final position – left transitory side stance LS (oi-dachi). During the unwinding of the body, the arms have changed their positions as a short block-punch has been performed with the edge of the palm along with the lower part of the left arm. Simultaneously, the trailing leg has slipped closer to the lead leg. Thus the whole position is now the same as at the beginning. With this combination 2A is completed, and we are ready for the next start.

Please, cut out this part along the indicated line and the edge of the photo in order to obtain the correct overview of the combination

✂ ─────

53
Initial
side stance
(oi-dachi)

54
Preliminary
step

60
Chambering for
front straight
thrust kick

Combination 4A

Fig. 53:
Initial position: left transitory side stance LS (Oi-dachi).

Fig. 54:
End of the first phase: right transitory reverse stance (compare fig. 26).

Fig. 60:
About one-third of phase two. While the position of the arms remains unchanged, after the start, the knee of the left attacking leg has been lifted into a high front position – the leg flexed – adopting the chambering position for a straight thrust kick to be launched. The right, support leg is now beginning a pushing-extending-twisting motion, thereby delivering additional acceleration to the forward-moving body, particularly on the left side, thus initiating the launching.

Please, cut out this part along the indicated line and the edge of the photo in order to obtain the correct overview of the combination

61	62	58	59
Front straight thrust kick (oi-mae-geri)	Rechambering and bending	Reverse fist punch (gyaku-tsuki)	Finishing-off: straight block (oi-shuto)

Fig. 61:
About two-thirds of phase two. This is the climax of the front straight thrust kick (oi-mae-geri) with the left foot to the body. The final acceleration emanates from the forward movement of the whole body, the strong pushing forward of the left hip – which gives a false impression that the upper body is leaning backwards – and the snapping extension of the left leg. The body is unwound, the left side turned in the direction of the attack, the arms keeping the corresponding transitory hold.

Fig. 62:
Approximately four-fifths of phase two. While the attacking left lower leg has been rechambered, the shoulders and arms have bent for the follow-up fist punch to be initiated by the turning of the support foot with its heel outwards.

Fig. 58:
End of the second phase. The climax of the right reverse fist punch to the body (gyaku-tsuki-chudan).

Fig. 59:
End of the phase three. Final position – left transitory side stance LS (oi-dachi). Combination 4A is now completed, and we are ready for the next start.

Please, cut out this part
along the indicated line and
the edge of the photo in
order to obtain the correct
overview of the
combination

53
*Initial
side stance
(oi-dachi)*

54
*Preliminary
step*

63
*Launching position
for a straight sweep*

Combination 6A

Fig. 53:
Initial position: left transitory side stance LS (oi-dachi).

Fig. 54:
End of the first phase: right transitory reverse stance (compare fig. 26) in preparation for the start of a sweeping attack.

Fig. 63:
About one-third of phase two. While the position of the arms remains unchanged, the attacking left leg has been lifted slightly sideways after the start and is slightly flexed for a launching position for the sweep-attack to follow.

Please, cut out this part along the indicated line and the edge of the photo in order to obtain the correct overview of the combination

64	65	58	59
Straight sweep (ko-soto-gari)	Rechambering and bending	Reverse fist punch (gyaku-tsuki)	Finishing-off: straight block (oi-shuto)

Fig. 64:
About two-thirds of phase two. The climax of the left straight sweep with a hook-formed leg attacking the opponent's lead leg (ko-soto-geri). The final acceleration emanates from the sweeping movement of the attacking leg as well as from the left side of the body moving forward – like falling onto the imaginary opponent.

Fig. 65:
Approximately four-fifths of phase two. We have explosively pulled our striking leg into the front chambering position, thus preventing ourselves from falling forward; the left body side – the shoulder leading – has been driven forward extensively, while the right shoulder and arm are in a launching position for the fist punch, which is just being introduced by the right heel turning outwards.

Fig. 58:
End of the second phase. Climax of the right reverse fist punch to the body (gyaku-tsuki-chudan).

Fig. 59:
End of the phase three. Final position – left transitory side stance LS (oi-dachi) with a straight block. Combination 6A is completed. We are ready for the next start.

71

Please, cut out this part
along the indicated line and
the edge of the photo in
order to obtain the correct
overview of the
combination

53	54	66
Initial	*Preliminary*	*Rechambering for a*
side stance	*step*	*front straight*
(oi-dachi)		*roundhouse kick*

Combination 8A

Fig. 53:
Initial position: left transitory side stance LS (oi-dachi).

Fig. 54:
End of the first phase: right transitory reverse stance. Preliminary step is finished while the upper body is wringing further, the left shoulder and arm are leading, thus introducing the start of the left foot attack.

Fig. 66:
About one-third of phase two. Chambering: after the start, the left knee has been explosively pulled extremely high in front of the chest, the lower leg is flexed in the launch position for a front straight roundhouse kick. While the position of the shoulders and arms remain unchanged, the body has just begun to incline backwards, and the right, support leg is just beginning the push-extension-twist motion, thus initiating the launching of the roundhouse kick.

Please, cut out this part along the indicated line and the edge of the photo in order to obtain the correct overview of the combination

67	68	58	59
Front straight roundhouse kick (oi-mawashi-geri)	*Rechambering and bending*	*Reverse fist punch (gyaku-tsuki)*	*Finishing-off: straight block (oi-shuto)*

Fig. 67:
About two-thirds of phase two. The climax of the left front straight roundhouse kick (oi-mawashi-geri) to the head. The final acceleration emanates from a synergy of the leaning backward of the upper body, the pushing-extending-twisting of the right leg, which has been transferred onto the hip and attacking leg, and from the lifting and snapping extension of the kicking leg. The position of the head serves here to keep the balance and visual control over the action. The position of the shoulders and arms remains unchanged i.e., in the direction of the follow-up attack.

Fig. 68:
Approximately four-fifths of phase two. Rechambering with an explosive retraction of the lower leg back into the flexed position, simultaneously twisting the thigh upwards and keeping the knee high, supporting the straightening up of the upper body. The arms and shoulders are now bending to their extreme for a hand attack which will be initiated by the right heel turning outwards.

Fig. 58:
End of the second phase. Climax of the right reverse fist punch to the body (gyaku-tsuki-chudan).

Fig. 59:
End of the phase three. Final position – left transitory side stance LS (oi-dachi). Combination 8A is now finished. We are ready for the next start.

53	69	70	71	72
Initial side stance (oi-dachi)	*Cross-step*	*Turning hips and legs*	*Preliminary step*	*Chambering for back (straight) side kick*

Combination 10A

Fig. 53:
Initial position: left transitory side stance LS (oi-dachi).

Fig. 69:
About one-third of phase one. With the left leg, we cross over the fighting axis, thus introducing a half-turn.

Fig. 70:
About two-thirds of phase one. Turning of the legs and hips through nearly 180 degrees on the balls of the feet has just finished. However, the shoulders and arms remain in the same position and at the same angle as the direction of the attack.

Fig. 71:
End of phase one: backward right transitory reverse stance. We have just made a backward step towards the imaginary opponent in order to prepare the body for a backwards side thrust kick.

Fig. 72:
Approximately one-third of phase two. After the start, we have explosively chambered the attacking leg into the launching position, thereby keeping the position of the upper body as it was before.

Please, cut out this part along the indicated line and the edge of the photo in order to obtain the correct overview of the combination

73	74	58	59
Backward (straight) side kick (yoko-ushiro-geri)	*Reverting, rechambering and bending*	*Reverse fist punch (gyaku-tsuki)*	*Finishing-off: straight block (oi-shuto)*

Fig. 73:
About two-thirds of phase two. The climax of the left backwards (straight) side kick (yoko-ushiro-geri) to the body. The final acceleration emanates from a synergy of the sudden inclination of the upper body downwards, the extension of the support leg, the pushing-off of the hips in the direction of the attack, and from the extending and lifting of the attacking leg. The position of the shoulders and arms in relation to the direction of attack remain unchanged.

Fig. 74:
Approximately four-fifths of phase two. Rechambering the kicking leg by snapping the lower leg back and simultaneously twisting the thigh upwards. This has supported the straightening up of the body. The shoulders and arms are bending for the hand attack, which is to be introduced by the right heel turning outwards.

Fig. 58:
End of the second phase. Climax of the right reverse fist punch to the body (gyaku-tsuki-chudan).

Fig. 59:
End of the phase three. Final position – left transitory side stance LS (oi-dachi). Combination 10A is thus finished. We are ready for the next start.

53	69	70	71	75
Initial	*Cross-step*	*Turning*	*Preliminary*	*Launching position*
side stance		*hips and*	*step*	*for back reverted*
(oi-dachi)		*legs*		*roundhouse kick*

Combination 12A

Fig. 53:
Initial position: left transitory side stance LS (oi-dachi).

Fig. 69:
About one-third of phase one. With the left leg, we cross over the fighting axis, thus intro-ducing a half-turn.

Fig. 70:
About two-thirds of phase one. Turning of the legs and hips through nearly 180 degrees on the ball of the left foot has just finished. The shoulders and arms remain in the same position and at the same angle as the direction of the attack.

Fig. 71:
End of phase one: backward right transitory reverse stance. We have just made a backward step towards the imaginary opponent in order to prepare the body for starting the intended kick.

Fig. 75:
About one-third of phase two. After the start, we have lifted the slightly flexed attacking leg a little sideways into a launching position for the back reverted (straight) roundhouse kick to follow – it has been introduced by the leaning of the body.

76	77	58	59
Back reverted (straight) roundhouse kick (ura-mawashi-geri)	Reverting, rechambering and bending for the punch	Reverse fist punch (gyaku-tsuki)	Finishing-off: straight block (oi-shuto)

Fig. 76:
Approximately two-thirds of phase two. The climax of the back reverted (straight, though mostly called 'reverse') roundhouse kick (ura-mawashi-geri) to the head. The final acceleration emanates from a synergy of the intensive inclination of the body sideways and down, the extension of the support leg, the resultant lifting of the left hip, and from the work of the leg muscles while lifting and backward swinging, followed by a partial snapping of the attacking leg backwards. The position of the shoulders and arms, relative to the direction of the attack, remain unchanged.

Fig. 77:
About four-fifths of phase two. After the impact (here imaginary), we have rechambered the kicking leg by an explosive snapping back of the lower leg along the path of the attack away from the target, and simultaneously turned the thigh upwards. This has supported the straightening up of the body. The shoulders and arms are bending for the follow-up hand attack, which is introduced by the right heel turning outwards.

Fig. 58:
End of the second phase. The climax of the right reverse fist punch into the body (gyaku-tsuki-chudan).

Fig. 59:
End of phase three. Final position – left transitory side stance LS (oi-dachi) with a finishing-off block. Combination 12A is thus completed. We are ready for the next start.

TACTICAL COMPONENTS

In order to illustrate the tactical components we will use the same principles as those presented when covering the technical groundwork. Each time we presuppose an ideal situation: our opponent does exactly that and only that which is suitable for the tactical execution of a certain predetermined technique.

The sequence of events in sports combat is extremely complex. It consists of individual engagements with pauses between them, not taking into consideration also the interruptions from referees. Individual engagements consist of fighting situations which are multi-layered in relation to the tactical possibilities, and change more or less unpredictably. Individual fighting actions are therefore constantly being unexpectedly interrupted, or, become changed because of the requirement to make rapid adjustments to new fighting situations. For our purposes, we should reduce and simplify this complexity as follows.

The engagement is the basic unit of any fighting sequence, and it signifies the course of fighting activities of both competitors between two tactical breaks; it can also coincide with tactical intervals regulated by the referees. A tactical break happens when the flow of activity naturally stops due either to technical unviability or tactical senselessness in carrying out further actions, or, when the referee interrupts the fighting.

Let us imagine an ideal, complete engagement, which is of course in reality a rather exceptional occurrence. It is composed of the following four consecutive tactical phases:
- ◆ preparation for the attack
- ◆ initiation of the attack
- ◆ execution of the attack
- ◆ finishing-off the attack

We apply this classification when analyzing various tactics used in combat. Some of them are used during the whole combat, while others are only used occasionally under specific conditions. We are talking primarily about two groups of tactics: passive protective tactics and active fighting tactics. In order to be able to observe and clearly discern the movements of the legs and arms in relation to the attacks of the opponent, we must apply the principle of slow-motion. The movements happen otherwise with such lightning speed, suddenly and unexpectedly, so that we would be unable to discern all the basic components of any single tactic.

The Tactical Structure of Fighting

Tactical Moment as the Aim of Fighting

To present the technical components of our fighting repertoire in their pure form, we have imagined an ideal fighting situation: The opponent, standing in front of us, is not assuming a fighting stance – i.e., he/she is not protecting him-/herself with his/her arms and is behaving, on the whole, passively since he/she:

♦ is not attacking as we initiate our attack;
♦ does not counter-attack as we execute our attack;
♦ is not evading our attack;
♦ is not trying to prevent our attack with a block or deflection.

Consequently, our opponent is, by and large, totally incapable of fighting since he/she is unable to start any fighting action at all. Thus he/she is in a state which we call a *state of reduced ability to start*, abbreviated – *RAS*. At the same time, we are standing away from the opponent, still just within the range of our intended attack and ready to start it (see fig. 100, Spatial variables of attacks, p. 94).

This kind of situation we call a *tactical moment*, abbreviated – *TM*. TM refers not just to the dimension of time, i.e., to a moment, but to the whole situation. The ideal situation we described above, in presenting the technical components, is of course a state of an uninterrupted, total TM.

In actual sports combat, both competitors – fighter (White) and his/her opponent (Red) – are trying to achieve the same goal, that is, to hit an opponent's vital points successfully. To this end, they must first actively establish a TM or at least stimulate its creation. This is equally difficult for both of them; each of them has to protect him-/herself from the opponent's attacks, while at the same time continuously trying to maintain a high degree of readiness to attack. Each of the two fighters tries to initiate his/her attack in such a way that at the moment when he/she actually attacks, the opponent is in a state of RAS. This is the goal of every single engagement in each combat bout.

Types of Tactical Moments

There are two main types of TM: (a) latent TMs, and (b) evident TMs.

Latent TMs are those states of RAS which are difficult to recognize, yet which invariably happen with all fighters from time to time at certain intervals. Whether or not a latent TM was to the benefit of White can only be determined by the success or failure of White's attack. A latent TM occurs because a fighter:

- is not able to concentrate with the same intensity the whole time;
- is focusing his/her attention on an attack that seems most probable at a certain moment but which is in fact different from the attack his/her opponent intends to launch;
- is not able to keep his/her muscles tensed all the time, ready to start, and has to relax them from time to time;
- must also breathe and during inhalation is not fully able to start.

The RAS states are more recognizable – and last longer – the more a fighter's will to fight is weakened. This happens according to the degree he/she:

- is out of breath;
- is tired or exhausted;
- has pains;
- is afraid;
- has lost his/her self-confidence.

Evident TMs are those RAS states which are recognizable, and can be predicted. These states of RAS occur most often while the fighter is moving in the fighting area; they occur practically in all four tactical phases, and are especially evident during tactical maneuvering. While moving in the fighting area, the fighter is transferring his/her body weight from one leg onto the other in a more or less distinctive manner. This transfer has the following phases:

- readiness for start (balance);
- decision to start;
- start – beginning of weight transfer;
- labile period;
- weight transfer from one foot to the other in the desired direction; this can consist also of an attack with a hand or foot, or both;
- touch-down of the moving foot – end of weight transfer;
- orientation in the new body position.

Although each of these phases (as well as all of them together) can be very short and even difficult to discern (as in slight moves), none of them can be left out. While transferring weight, the fighter's capability for starting something new, i.e., to make a change to the action just being performed, is significantly reduced. Until his balance is regained, the fighter can only evade or prevent an attack of the opponent in a limited way – that is, by ducking or bending the upper body left or right, or by blocking or deflecting. In such a case the more the body or arm movements disturb the weight transfer, the harder it is to be successful to evade or prevent the opponent's attack.

The more extensively the fighter changes his/her stance or position the more the whole maneuver is predetermined and fixed, and the harder it is to change it in order to attack in another direction.

We also divide TMs according to which vital points are exposed. This then also defines which type of attack (I–VI), and the height (head, body) one can attack. During a state of RAS, more then one vital point is usually exposed, which gives the attacker a better choice in selecting the kind of attack, and, a greater probability of success.

Exploiting the Tactical Moment

The appearance of a TM is of no significant importance for a fighter unless he/she has exploited it with an actual attack. Similar to the subdivision of TMs into latent and evident ones, there are also two main sorts of attacks: (a) blind attacks and (b) planned attacks.

Blind attacks are those in which White attacks Red without previously perceiving the creation of a RAS with Red, or those in which White did not try to induce the creation of a TM. Such attacks are basically conducted in the hope of an erroneous reaction on the part of Red, and for the occurrence of a TM coinciding with this, or at least with the following attack. A blind attack is a way of inducing the occurrence of a TM. Blind attacks can be successful under the following conditions:

- ◆ one of the latent TMs must occur simultaneously with the attack, or the attack must provoke such a reaction by the opponent so that it leads to a creation of a TM.
- ◆ exploitation of a TM with an appropriate attack technique is necessary, and a must; the attack has to be directed towards the vital point which is exposed and not to one which may be protected or unreachable.

A blind attack has a better chance of success if the opponent is either surprised, or not experienced enough to react properly. This is very important, however, since not knowing how the opponent will react, the attacker is putting him-/herself in a rather uncertain situation. In the middle of an attack, the attacker is him-/herself in a state of RAS for other actions which might be necessary if the opponent reacts correctly and counter-attacks.

If a TM appears as a result of a blind attack, then the follow-on attack is considered to be planned. A planned attack is one in which the attacker can expect, with a high degree of certainty, that a TM will occur during the execution of the attack. Planned attacks are successful under the following conditions:

- the attacker must be able to anticipate precisely when the opponent will be in a state of RAS.
- the anticipated state of RAS must actually occur, while the attacker is both at an appropriate distance for an attack and ready to launch it, thus creating a TM.
- the TM created in this way must be exploited with an appropriate attack.

The probability that an attack will not be successful due to incorrect anticipation regarding the occurrence of a TM is rather high. However, in our fighting repertoire the possibility of such a failure is reduced by using combined consecutive attacks. Because the attacker has been trained, he should ostensibly be able to continue technically after the first, unsuccessful attack, directly with a follow-up one. Tactically, the first, unsuccessful attack fulfills an important task: it forces the opponent into changing his/her stance or position, i.e., forcing him into a state of RAS and, consequently, creating a TM for the next attack. Serial attacks serve their purpose providing the following conditions are fulfilled:

- after every attack, the attacker must be technically ready to start a new one;
- after the previous unsuccessful attack, the opponent should not be outside the attacker's range.

We also differentiate attacks tactically by various possible fighting situations:

- regarding the way the fight is conducted, there are:
  - trapping attacks when the attacker has caught the opponent in a state of RAS in the middle of maneuvering or in retreat;
  - intercepting counter-attacks when the opponent has surprised the attacker in a state of RAS in the middle of his/her own attack.
- regarding tactical angles, in which the attack on the opponent is performed, there are:
  - direct attacks along the existing fighting axis and –
  - attacks from the side or side attacks, which happen on either side of the opponent.
- regarding the exposure of the vital points which are being attacked there are:
  - attacks with a frontal hit, and –
  - attacks with a hit from a side.

Guidelines for Fighting Tactics

Our tactical behavior during sports combat follows two basic guidelines: (a) deception or feinting, and (b) active prosecution of the fight, which we also refer to as dictating the tempo and/or mode of fighting, i.e., taking the initiative.

"Readiness to fight" refers to the general ability of a fighter to participate in a sports combat, while "readiness to start" means principally that a fighter is ready to act in accordance with a given fighting situation. Principally, a fighter is ready to act in a certain direction, within a certain time interval, and in a certain way, depending on how he/she perceives the given situation and expects it to develop. The more the actual action of the fighter White differs from the expectations of his/her opponent Red, the less Red is capable of correct action or reaction. Hence, the more White succeeds in bluffing or deceiving Red regarding his/her intentions, the bigger will be the effect of surprise and, with that, the time interval of the state of RAS when Red is vulnerable to attacks.

White can also create a reduced starting ability of his/her opponent Red by active prosecution of the fight, by exerting pressure, with changing threats of certain attacks, and by pretend or actual attacks, White forces Red into changes of stance and position, thus creating states of RAS. The more often this happens, and the more active and intrusive White is, the less opportunity Red has to maintain or re-establish his/her readiness to start his/her own actions and to take over the initiative.

Actively prosecuting the fight also includes provoking and misleading the opponent into attack, thus creating the illusion that the opponent has the initiative. In this way White is actually 'actively waiting' for an opportunity when Red, by attacking, creates the state of his/her RAS.

Components of Fighting Tactics

There are two main tactics used in combat: (a) protective or safeguarding tactics and (b) action oriented or active tactics.

It is no accident that protective tactics have been mentioned first here. As we have already indicated, even the attacker in action is exposed to counter-attacks, as long as the following conditions exist:

- ◆ the attacker has wrongly estimated the fighting situation – or has attacked just blindly – while no RAS has appeared on the side of the defender.
- ◆ during an attack, the attacker is also in a state of RAS.
- ◆ the defender is ready to start and is – because he is being attacked – at the right distance for a counter-attack.

In the case above, a TM occurs to the benefit of the defender. Many fighters utilize this way of creating TMs and become specialists in counter-attacks. Thus, any attacker has to be prepared for such surprises while attacking and consequently use protective tactics, such as:

- ◆ correct fighting stance (guard);
- ◆ invisible breathing;
- ◆ consistent protective position of the arms, as far as possible also during an attack;

- minimizing – or, alternatively, maximizing – gestures and motions when changing stance or position;
- prevention of hits by deflections, blocks, or bars.

Regardless of whether one is attacking or counter-attacking, it pays to maintain protection before, during, and after the attack.

Active tactics include all kinds of actions, such as those intended to mislead the opponent (feinting) as well as those used for active fighting:

- preparatory maneuvering in the bout area, comprising changes of stances and positions, circling and turning, as well as feinting gestures;
- all attacks introducing actions which serve to bridge distances, to establish a favorable stance or position for a particular attack, or to neutralize the opponent's holding of arms for protection – blocking or deflecting;
- execution of attacks to match individual situations;
- controlling the opponent with a block after an attack.

Protective Measures

Fighting Stance

A fighting stance is a special stance with a double function: (a) the guarding of the vital points against surprise attacks in the most effective way possible, and (b) the most explosive start possible for introducing an attack or any other fighting action necessary.

While moving through the bout area, all sorts of fighting stances can be applied. Most of these we can make by turning on the spot, as if we were surrounded by many opponents; this is displayed in figures 84 to 90, p. 85. Other fighting stances are also possible. However, we will not consider them here because they are all of a transitory nature.

The correct fighting stance is called the initial fighting stance, which we also term "guard". It differs from a technical or transitory stance, which we have seen in our presentation of basic combinations, in the following ways:

- We hold the arms in a basic protective or safeguarding posture. We hold the hands in front of the torso so that we directly cover some of the vital points, especially the solar plexus; other points are thereby guarded indirectly simply by the fact that the hands are able, over the shortest distance, to

78   79   80   81   82   83

Fig. 78–80:
Left initial side fighting stance
(oi-kumite-dachi)

Fig. 81–83:
Left initial reverse fighting stance
(gyaku-kumite-dachi)

84   85   86

Fig. 84–90:
Intermediate fighting stances
By turning on the spot we go through many known forms of intermediate fighting stances. During combat, while actively changing postures and positioning, a multitude of transitional fighting stances naturally occur, especially during preparatory maneuvering, and introducing actions. A good fighter tends the whole time to preserve the guarding posture of the arms.

87

90   89   88

intercept and deflect attacks directed toward those vital points. The palms are open, the edge of the lead hand faces forward, while the palm of the other hand is facing upwards (the back of the hand is turned toward the floor) with the fingers straight and pointing toward the opponent. The elbows are pointing toward the floor, the arms are partially bent and are relatively relaxed.

♦ The legs are positioned so that we are ready for a start and are simultaneously partially guarding the genitals with the thighs.

As for the position of the whole body, there are two main forms of the initial fighting stance: (a) the side stance and (b) the reverse stance (see fig. 78–80 and 81–83, p. 85).

Each of these two options has its advantages and disadvantages regarding both the guarding and the starting function. The side stance protects better, because the body is turned half away from the opponent, while in the reverse stance the body is turned frontal toward the opponent. On the other hand, the reverse fighting stance is better for starting than the side fighting stance.

One of the variations of the fighting stance is also the finishing-off or controlling stance, which we use for the completion of an attack in a clinch situation with the opponent. By applying the controlling stance we prevent any further activity of the opponent in the following way:

♦ by controlling his/her body and arms, which we bar (shut, lock) with our hands as much as possible; how we execute this kind of block depends on the given situation;

♦ by controlling his/her balance by leaning with a part of our body weight on him/her, thus being ready for a new start; should the opponent try to escape we immediately start another attack (fig. 168–177, p. 127).

Invisible Breathing

To prevent the opponent from noticing when we are not ready to start due to the rhythm of our breathing – hence, when we are in a state of RAS – during a fight we breathe in a manner so that it is invisible. The opponent must not be able to recognize when we inhale and when we exhale. We achieve this by breathing with the diaphragm and we do not raise the shoulders while breathing. In particular we must mask when we are out of breath. In such a situation we breath deeply, with a slightly open mouth and simultaneously through the nose, as is the usual habit in sports. We also try to slow down the breathing as rapidly as possible.

During the explosive exhalation with the combat shout (Kiai ! – as in the Japanese terminology) which accompanies the final phase of the attack, by contraction of all the participating muscles, especially the stomach muscles, we never exhale completely. We retain some air for a possible attack to follow. If we execute more attacks in a sequence, we inhale briefly during the introductory or preliminary phases of individual attacks.

Consequent Protection and the Minimizing of Gestures

Since they occur automatically due to a loss of concentration and muscle relaxation, we cannot avoid latent states of RAS. All we can do is to keep an appearance of a permanent readiness to start by consistently keeping the correct fighting stance, thus not allowing the states, mentioned above, to become physically visible.

When introducing a hand strike, the arms should bend for the punch as late and as fast as possible. By doing this, we conceal our intention to attack, and our protective hand posture is maintained until the last moment. During the punch, the lead hand is not pulled back in the manner we have seen in our presentation of technical components. Instead, the hand is kept in a protective position, unless it is already occupied with the controlling of the opponent's protection, or with the deflecting of a counter-attack (see e.g. fig. 181–184, p. 129).

Gestures, which happen during changes of stances while we are moving in the fighting area, we execute as quickly and economically as possible. We only perform functionally unavoidable gestures and movements. Every change of a protective posture, which serves for relaxation, correction of balance or for the introduction of some new attack, must be executed as fast and as minimally as possible. If it is possible, all such gestures should be executed simultaneously to maneuvering through the fighting area – provided this fits in with the attack – we move our legs as quickly and as little as possible, while keeping the guarding posture as intact as possible.

The alternative to minimizing gestures is to go to the other extreme and maximize our movements when changing stances or positions. This makes the opponent unsure about what is actually happening. However, such tactics belong to feinting and can be counted already as one of the active tactics.

Interception and Deflection

We understand interception and deflection as two parts of a gesture with an arm. First we intercept the opponent's strike, then immediately afterward, divert it so that in passing the target it runs out into nothing.

We can best intercept an attacking hand or foot with a part of the arm below the elbow, including the muscular part of our palm, by performing a half circular striking motion with the arm. After the intercepting contact, the protecting arm strikes strongly through and diverts the opponent's approaching arm or leg past the targeted vital area. After the deflection, if possible, we keep control over the opponent's arm or leg by forming a hook with the palm of the protecting hand, thus preventing the opponent's arm or leg from being pulled back immediately.

We differentiate between four kinds of possible deflections, depending on the vertical and horizontal directions of the hand movement (fig. 91–99, p. 89): upward or downward (relating to the position of the elbow of the deflecting arm); outward (away from the chest toward the shoulder of the deflecting arm); or inward (from the shoulder of the deflecting arm toward the chest). Here we will use some abbreviations:

- ◆ up-out: deflection upward-and-outward (age-soto-uke);
- ◆ up-in: deflection upward-and-inward (age-uchi-uke);
- ◆ down-out: deflection downward-and-outward (otoshi-soto-uke);
- ◆ down-in: deflection downward-and-inward (otoshi-uchi-uke).

Both hands can also perform deflections simultaneously, in which case, we have two possibilities:

- ◆ parallel, for example, A-up-in, B-up-out (morote-sukui-uke);
- ◆ crossing, for example, A-up-in, B-down-out (jiyu-sukui-uke).

In the first example, both arms are deflecting the same attack. Most often, however, it happens that the first hand has intercepted a strike and the second hand takes over to complete the deflection – which then frees the first hand for a counter-attack. In the second example, both hands are moved in the same direction, one up and one down – thereby protecting the whole side of the body, because the target for the strike is not yet known.

Interception and deflection are not just passive defensive measures, they can also be used to actively initiate counter-attacks. When we divert the attacking arm or leg away from its target, and possibly even control it for a moment, we create a state of RAS with the opponent. With the interception, the defender has also simultaneously bent his/her shoulders and arms for an attack, which he/she can immediately utilize. Interceptions, which develop into deflections, and/or controls, can be used with equal success as preparation for one's own attack: In this way, the opponent's guarding arm position can be moved away and/or controlled while simultaneously we are bending the shoulders and arms for our own punch (compare figures 120–167, p. 114–125). The active use of deflections or controls (bars) is also an essential part of the finishing-off of an attack.

Deflection up-out
(age-soto)

Deflection up-in
(age-uchi)

92   94

93

95

91

97

99

96   98

Deflection down-out
(otoshi-soto)

Deflection down-in
(otoshi-uchi)

Fig. 91–99: Interception and deflection *(sukui-uke)*

Here, we show the first two phases only (before and after the contact with the attacking arm or leg) of the first part of a deflection, that is, interception. The second part, the actual deflection, is performed – if possible – simultaneously with our counter-attack, as illustrated with various cases in the third chapter (see fig. 120–160).

89

Fighting Actions

Spatial categories – bounds, positions, distances and angles – are of crucial importance in explaining individual fighting actions and for understanding their mutual differences. To explain spatial concepts, we will again use our ideal fighting situation, as presented in figure 100, p. 94. This fighting situation has the following characteristics:

- ◆ attacker X attacks with a basic foot-hand combination which he/she is starting from the maximum possible distance of two strides.
- ◆ opponent Y is not counter-attacking. Attacker X is able to hit him/her with both strikes because Y, after being hit by X's kick, has moved backward, just enough so that X's hand-thrust can reach and hit him/her.
- ◆ it is also possible that Y has tried to evade the foot attack by moving one step to the right of the fighting axis; nevertheless the kick still hits him/her, but in this case, there is no second attack with the hand.
- ◆ similarly it is possible that Y might have evaded the kick by moving one step to the left of the fighting axis, in which case, he/she is then hit by the hand-thrust.

The last two possibilities of evasion by opponent Y – to the left and to the right of the fighting axis – are needed in order to illustrate the spatial variables of an attack with the foot, as distinct from the spatial variables of an attack with the hand. Details are shown in the legend at figure 100. A little later (fig. 105–106, p 97), we will also use some other spatial concepts which are necessary for the exact description of fighting actions.

Preparatory Actions

a) Description

In the preparation phase, we generate a situation in which we expect a TM to occur. During preparation, we approach the opponent at a distance from which it is possible to launch an attack when it appears that a TM will occur. In this phase, the following actions are mutually intertwined:

- ◆ a change of position along the fighting axis, with the help of steps or sliding;
- ◆ a change of position left or right of the fighting axis by circling or turning (fig. 101–104, p. 96);
- ◆ a change of stance from a side stance into a reverse stance and vice versa, or by changing the feet or by turning while keeping the arms intact in the guarding position.

b) Application

The tactical goal of this phase is to provoke the occurrence of a TM, which we are trying to achieve by forcing our opponent to move across the bout area. Since the opponent is pursuing the same tactical goal – which is to reach a TM, but to his/her benefit – his/her reactions to our preparatory actions are consequently, to a certain degree, predictable and dirigible.

For example, the attacker in our illustration (here designated with X) is trying to move to the side, in order to generate a tactical angle (compare the explanation to fig. 100), which would enable him/her to attack from the side. The opponent Y will most likely try to prevent this by making a complementary move and thus neutralize the developing tactical angle. Alternatively, he/she will try to utilize this tactical angle for his/her own attack (see fig.105–106, p. 97). After several repetitions of the same maneuver, attacker X will be able to anticipate – with a fair degree of certainty regarding direction, speed, timing, and duration – that there is a state of RAS with opponent Y. What he/she must then do, is to be in that moment at an appropriate distance to attack (see table 3, p. 112), and, technically be able to initiate the attack.

The preparation of an attack is possible somewhere between two diametrically opposed practical approaches:

- The attacker acts with minimum moves and gestures, while his/her opponent is moving across the bout area rather extensively; the attacker is actually waiting for the opponent to get into a state of RAS thus generating a TM to his/her own disadvantage.
- The attacker is maneuvering extensively and gesticulating a lot, thus becoming completely unpredictable to the opponent; the opponent becomes confused and reacts in a disorganized manner so that various TMs are likely to occur.

Introductory Actions

a) Description

The introductory phase is the most important phase of an engagement. Whether or not the attack will be successful depends on its introduction. The introduction comprises all the actions called preliminary, initial, or introducing actions, which are made in that very short time interval between the anticipation of a TM and its actual occurrence. In this short time, the attacker must reach the right distance and take up the proper position for launching the attack. If the anticipated TM actually appears, the attack is launched (compare the explanation with figure 100), and if not, it is still possible to continue with some other action, as required by the new fighting situation.

The introduction of an attack, up until the moment of launching, consists of tactical and technical introductory moves and gestures, which we will, from now on, differentiate as follows:

- ◆ Tactical introductory actions are composed of the following actions:
  - bridging the distance to the opponent until one is in range for an attack by:
    - − leap or shift
    - − lunge or pre-jump
    - − spring or stride
  - forming of tactical angles to attack from the side by:
    - − slide to the side
    - − changeover of leading leg with a side-step
    - − leap to the side
  - removing the protecting arms by:
    - − interception/ blocking and deflection
- ◆ Technical introductory actions consist of:
  - taking up a posture to launch a foot attack by:
    - − straight start of the striking leg
    - − start with a cross-step over the striking axis
    - − start with a turn
    - − start with a counter-turn
  - taking up a posture to launch a hand attack by:
    - − bending shoulders and arms
    - − changing of hands and bending

Table 2 (p. 100) gives an overview of combining various bridging moves – up to the distance of one stride – with actions for taking a launching stance for a foot attack.

What we term here as a lunge or sally is an explosive movement of the lead foot forward (fig. 111, p. 101). A leap or shift means that the rear foot is shifted with a slight jump into a parallel position with the lead foot – whereby the front leg, in most cases, is lifted into a launching position (fig. 109, p.101). If after the jump we land ahead of where the lead leg was, this is called a pre-jump, and with this we reach the same striking distance as a lunge, that is, about half a normal stride. A spring is a longer lunge and bridges the distance of one whole stride.

A cross-over step is transferring the front leg over the other foot's axis of attack; with this, a better starting position is achieved for backward and semi-round kicks. For backward kicks we also need a counter- or half-turn, as well as the spin, turn or full-turn (see fig. 108, 110, 112, 114, p. 101). When the turn is made, the rear foot attacks, while in a counter-turn the front foot attacks, as viewed from the direction of the attack.

Technical initiating actions also have their tactical variations, because depending on the situation, the cross-over step can be bigger or smaller, and the turn or counter-turn more or less explicit depending on which angle we expect to have to launch the foot into the attack (kick). Technical and tactical introductory attacks are actually, in practice, very interwoven and blur into each other, so that usually we can hardly differentiate between them.

b) Application

Which of the above introductory actions we use, and in which sequence we apply them, depends on:
- distance to the actual or anticipated position of the opponent, at which the start begins;
- time in which we expect the opponent to get into a state of RAS;
- direction from which the opponent will move into a state of RAS;
- form and exposed side of the fighting stance from which we begin;
- type of the attack to follow.

The success of an introduction depends on the opponent's perception capacity, reaction time, and co-ordination capacity. First, he/she has to recognize what is actually happening, that is, that an attack has been initiated, and then he/she has also to modify his/her actions to cope with the attack. Therefore, the shorter one keeps the initiation phase, the greater are the possibilities of success. This requires a relatively short fighting distance, which enables us to perform blitz attacks with short introductions. However, the fighting distance must be large enough for the attacker to recognize his/her opponent's intentions in time.

In our experience, it is not meaningful for the introduction to last longer than it takes to bridge the gap of two strides. A really long – spatially and with regard to time – introduction usually occurs only when pursuing a retreating opponent. An introduction with two shifts of the foot, which is technically equal to two strides, is used in sideways counter-attacks. In these cases, the tactical and technical introductions fuse, which significantly shortens the duration of the introduction. The most commonly used introduction consists of one stride or one shift of the foot. In a direct counter-attack, when our opponent is approaching to launch his/her own attack, we do not need to tactically bridge the distance.

Fig. 100: Spatial variables of attacks

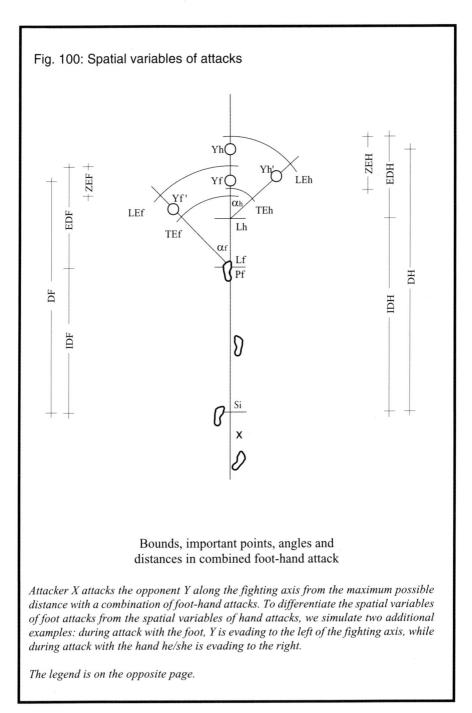

Bounds, important points, angles and
distances in combined foot-hand attack

*Attacker X attacks the opponent Y along the fighting axis from the maximum possible
distance with a combination of foot-hand attacks. To differentiate the spatial variables
of foot attacks from the spatial variables of hand attacks, we simulate two additional
examples: during attack with the foot, Y is evading to the left of the fighting axis, while
during attack with the hand he/she is evading to the right.*

The legend is on the opposite page.

Legend to fig. 100: Spatial variables of attacks

X – Attacker
Y – Opponent

Bounds:
TEf – Threshold of Effectiveness of Foot attack; the line at which a foot attack begins to gain sufficient effect.
LEf – Limit of Effectiveness of Foot attack; the line which ends the zone where the foot attack is effective, i.e., it designates the foot attack range.
TEh – Threshold of Effectiveness of Hand attack; the line at which a hand attack begins to gain sufficient effect.
LEh – Limit of Effectiveness of Hand attack; the line which ends the zone where the hand attack is effective, i.e., it marks the hand attack range.

Positions:
Si – Starting point for introduction of attack; position of lead foot during start.
Pf – Push-off point of stand foot during foot attack execution.
Lf – Point of launching foot attack; it is identical with Pf.
Lh – Point of launching hand attack; regarding time and space, this is directly before the touchdown of the attacking foot.
Yf – Opponent's position within ZEF.
Yf' – Possible opponent's position after evasion to the right (from his/her point of view) of the fighting axis and still within ZEF.
Yh – Opponent's position within ZEH.
Yh' – Possible opponent's position after evasion to the left (from his/her point of view) and still within ZEH.

Angles:
αf – Tactical angle (of evasion) to Y's favour; simultaneously also the angle for which X must adjust his/her axis of foot attack before launching the kick.

αh – Tactical angle (of evasion) to Y's favour; simultaneously also the angle for which X must adjust his/her axis of hand attack before launching the punch.

Distances:
(all distances are measured on the ground)
DF – Distance for Foot attack: it is composed of IDF and EDF, as measured from the ball of the front foot (Si), before the introduction of attack up to the opponent's position Yf.
IDF– Introduction Distance for Foot attack: distance between the starting point for introduction (Si) and push-off point for execution of the attack (Pf = Lf): between 0 and maximum 2 strides.
EDF– Execution Distance for Foot attack: this depends on the opponent's position within the ZEF, as measured from the point of launching the kick (Lf) up to the attacked opponent's position Yf.
ZEF– Zone of Effectiveness of Foot-attack: distance between the threshold (TEf) and limit (LEf) of foot attack effectiveness.
DH – Distance for Hand attack: it consists of IDH and EDH.
IDH– Introduction Distance for Hand attack: it is measured from the starting point of introduction (Si), to the point of launching the hand attack (Lh).
EDH– Execution Distance for Hand attack: it depends on the opponent's position within ZEH, as measured from the point of launching a punch (Lh), to the opponent's position Yh.
ZEH– Zone of Effectiveness of Hand attack: the distance between the threshold (TEh) and limit (LEh) of hand attack effectiveness.

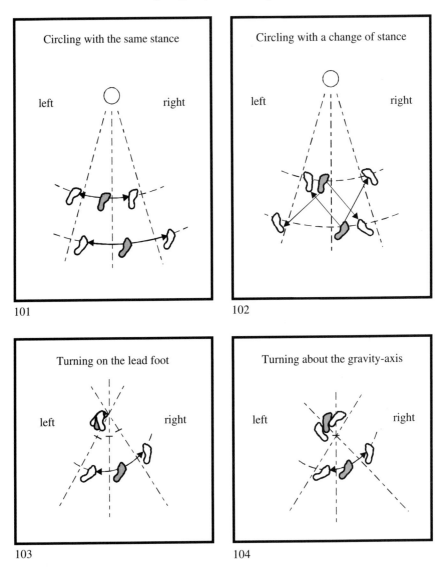

Fig. 101–104: Typical examples of circling and turning

Turning on the lead foot is a transition between circling and turning. Turning on the back foot is only of value if the most of our body weight is transferred onto the back leg. Simultaneously with turning, we can also change our stance.

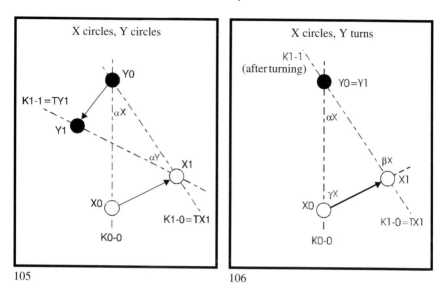

Fig. 105–106: Tactical situations after changing position to the side

Legend:

X	–	Attacker
Y	–	Defender
XO	–	Introductory position of X
X1	–	Position of X after the move
YO	–	Introducing position of Y
Y1	–	Position of Y after the move
αX	–	Tactical angle to X's favour
αY	–	Tactical angle to Y's favour
BX	–	Angle of X's attack
γX	–	Angle of X's movement

KO-O	–	Fighting axis at the starting positions of X and Y.
K1-O	–	Fighting axis after a change in the position of X.
K1-1	–	Fighting axis after a change in the position or turning of Y.
TX1	–	Tactical axis to X's favour.
TY1	–	Tactical axis to Y's favour

When attacker X is moving to the side, a favorable tactival angle will exist until opponent Y turns (fig. 106) or moves to the side in response (fig. 105). In the second case, opponent Y generates a tactically advantageous angle, thus taking over the initiative until attacker X adopts the new fighting axis.

97

Execution Actions

a) Description

During the execution phase, the tactical goal is to utilize a given TM and simultaneously, if the expected RAS of the opponent does not happen, to prevent the opponent from utilizing our own state of RAS – which occurs when we are in the course of our attack. In this phase, we launch an attack with the hand or foot from the launching position.

• Attack with the foot

When the six basic types of attacks with the foot are implemented in a sports bout, they have to be adjusted to concrete given situations. Many circumstances influence these adjustments.

Firstly, the speed, strength, and distinctiveness of the form of foot attacks depend to a great degree on how they were actually initiated in regard to the acceleration and the way of setting the striking leg into the launching posture. Further, how high we lift our leg and how much it will be extended during the kick depends on the actual distance to the opponent, as well as on the height of the targeted vital point. Furthermore, every change of the axis of attack during the initiation demands an adjustment of the attack. If the opponent has moved slightly to the side, for instance, then that requires either stronger or reduced turning on the standing leg.

• Attack with the hand

Attacks with the hand, presented in our basic combinations, have to be adapted to tactical requirements when applied in any concrete fighting situation. So, for instance, the distance to the opponent's vital point will determine the degree of extension of the attack arm. The zone of effectiveness of hand attacks can be quite large: it reaches from a short punch with an almost completely flexed arm (as in a clinch) to a fist punch with a fully extended arm.

If the opponent has evaded a foot attack by moving to the left or to the right, then the hand attack that follows has to be directed to the new position of the opponent. This can happen in the following two ways. While the attacking foot is pulled back and the arms are bending for the attack, we have to turn the whole body into the new direction on the standing leg. Alternatively, we extend the attack arm along the new axis of attack only. Usually, both methods are combined and used simultaneously.

Because of the need for effective and continuous protection of our own vital points, we change the guarding position of our arms into bending for a punch as late as possible. Also, during an attack with one hand, the other hand is kept as much and as long as possible in the guarding position. Thus, if needed, it can easily be activated, either to prevent a counter-attack or to remove the opponent's protection.

Besides the usual straight hand punch, which we execute along the opponent's guarding arm, controlled by our lead hand, we can also throw a hand punch directly over the opponent's guarding lead arm. This punch is more covert and the opponent is only able to see it when the fist appears above his/her guarding lead arm. Similar adjustments of the line of attacks, meant to avoid obstacles, are seen fairly often in contest practice. One of the most commonly seen adjustments occurs when the opponent hides his/her head between his/her raised shoulders. In this, and similar cases, the variations of hand strikes are suitable – implemented with the bottom or the back of the fist (like hammering) or with the edge of the palm (like cutting), etc.

It also happens that, for tactical reasons, the intended foot attack, or even the step, is to be dropped off as the striking distance has shortened suddenly. In such cases, we perform a hand punch without lunging forward, just applying some transfer of weight forward. Sometimes even this is not applicable.

Under normal circumstances, every attack has to be adapted to several tactical requirements at the same time. However, as long as the strikes are effective, there is no point in differentiating all the tactical requirements at issue.

b) Application

The attack implementation phase begins when the whole body is in a position ready to launch a foot attack, and when the acceleration for its launch has already been accumulated. Principally, we attack with a combination foot-hand. The kick initiates the hand strike not only technically, as we have seen in the technical presentation of combinations, but also tactically. Independent of whether the kick has hit its target or not, it usually causes either a prolongation of the actual TM or the generation of a new TM.

In cases when our opponent has evaded the foot attack by withdrawing outside of the range of our hand attack, but is still within the reach of an attack with the other foot, then we implement that second foot attack and, given the tactical conditions, apply the hand attack thereafter. In this way, we can execute a whole row of consecutive attacks until the flow of actions either is technically interrupted or becomes tactically meaningless. In such a case, the attack implementation phase is completed with the last strike. The opposite to this is the counter-attack, where we usually stop the action after one single strike or kick.

Introduction of attack from the left fighting stance				Technical introduction: adjustment of the body posture					
Tactical introduction: bridging of distance				no initia-tion	turn	coun-ter-turn	cross-step	cross-step + turn	cross-step + count-er-turn
Distance in normal steps	At-tack leg	Sup-port leg	Intro-ductory action						
0	R		no ini-tiation						
	L	R	leap/shift						
0 to 0,5	R	L	lunge						
	L	R	pre-jump						
0,5 to 1	R	L	spring						
	L	R	stride						

Table 2: Fusion of technical and tactical introductory actions

Every technical adjustment of the body can be made in connection with a tactical bridging of distance. Also, several tactical distance-bridging moves can be mutually combined when the distances are great.

107 No introduction; direct attack

108 Cross-step with counter-turn

109 Leap/ Shift

110 Leap with cross-step and counter-turn

Fig.107–114: Some examples of combined introductory actions

111 Lunge

112 Lunge with counter-turn

113 Step/Stride

114 Step/Stride with turn

Finishing-off Actions

a) Description

The tactical goal of the completion phase is to end the engagement in such a way that the opponent is unable to continue to fight, while at the same time the attacker remains in control of the situation. For this purpose, we use the already-mentioned technical variation of blocking that we adapt to the given situation, that is, to the position and movement of both fighters: a barring or blocking of the attacked opponent with a more or less extended arm, whereby the other hand is usually utilized as well, and a shorter or longer final stance with the attacker leaning on the opponent, more or less with the body weight. From the final stance, the attacker is capable of immediately continuing the fight, if necessary.

b) Application

Two main forms of ending actions are most useful. The first one is applied when the opponent retreats after the attack outside the range of the hand. In this case, the attacker finishes off by changing arms, thus only reinstating the punch launching posture which he/she then immediately transforms into an initial fighting stance, ready for a new engagement.

The second is applied when the attacked opponent stays where he/she has been at the time of the attack. In this case, the attacker has moved close to the opponent simply by the momentum of his/her attack. At the same time he/she transfers the backlash of the attack into a block-punch, barring with it the opponent's arms – or blocking them off, if his/her opponent has attempted a counter-attack. Simultaneously, if applicable, the attacker is trying to keep the opponent in an unstable state by leaning his/her body weight onto the opponent (compare fig. 168–177, p. 127).

Yet another, third form of ending action has often been applied at competitions. Namely, immediately after his/her attack, the attacker follows his/her natural reflex to get out of the zone of danger. Consequently, he/she pulls back with the side. The attacker moves the whole body away from the opponent thus getting out of reach of potential counter-attacks. However, as much as this finishing-off action seems at first glance to be most useful, it can easily become fatal for the attacker. If the main, last attack has not been successful – that is, there has been no hit – an alert opponent can quickly utilize this situation to his/her advantage. While the attacker is moving backward, considering the engagement to be finished, the opponent can launch a series of attacks, thus surprising the attacker, constraining him/her to continue retreating, and probably hitting him/her. Even if the attacker has shifted his/her arms while retreating, thus bending for a new attack, any introduction of a new attack – but particularly of a foot attack – has, under these circumstances, become more difficult. The attacker would have first to overcome the inertia of his/her backward movement before he/she could start to launch an attack again. Thus he/she has lost the initiative, which, if the referee does not stop the contest, can have negative consequences for him/her as just described.

Early forms of European karate-like fighting

An illustration from the book Fechtkunst *(The Art of Fighting) by J.A. Schmidt from 1713. The attacker is swinging for a strike by completely turning his shoulders; the opponent is holding his arms for protection as we see it also nowadays in karate competitions.*

Early forms of European
karate-like fighting

In the drawings below, from the book Fechtkunst *(The Art of Fighting) by J. A. Schmidt, 1713, each of the attackers swings an arm for a strike while holding the opponent at a distance with the opposite arm. We can observe that the left hand is held high, ready for a strike. The shoulder of the attacking side is completely turned in the direction of the attack. This natural fighting movement was in use in the ancient Occident as well as in the Orient and we can see it today occasionally also in sports karate tournaments. It is amazing that this well-known fighting technique has not found its way into the traditional karate schools, despite being in use for centuries also in Japan. Above: A drawing of a well-known gate-guardian statue, several metres tall, in one of the Japanese temples.*

3. APPLICATION OF THE FIGHTING REPERTOIRE IN SPORTS KARATE

FIGHTING IN PRACTICE

The Course of a Sports Bout

So far, we have become acquainted with the technical and tactical components of our sports fighting repertoire and seen their mutual interdependence. What we do in sports combat is fused together from these two basic components. Tactical feasibility determines how the applied techniques are performed, while technical viability limits the use of certain tactics.

In each single engagement – this being, as we know, the basic segment of a sports bout – we rarely go through all the tactical phases mentioned so far. It is rather the case that certain phases are left out or are repeated several times. The flow chart diagram (fig.115) illustrates the sequence of a sports bout. It shows the sequence, potential fusion, and possible repetitions, as well as the tactical phases omitted. For clarity's sake, we consider here only two possible interruptions by the referee. This diagram shows more clearly what we already know from experience: that at any point, the fighter X can decide, following his/her tactical feeling, whether to implement his/her intended action or, if considering it more suitable, move on to another one, omitting one or several phases, or returning to a previous phase or even repeating the same one. For example, if he was preparing a foot attack, he/she can:

- ◆ omit it and directly apply a hand attack, or:

- continue with a kick, or:
- finish-off immediately afterwards, but despite that, continue with a new attack, or:
- begin with maneuvering again.

During a bout, one can always expect it to be interrupted at any moment, either by the opponent or by the referee.

It is not intended in this book to present a more detailed description of all the ways how individual engagements can occur. Here, these possibilities can only be indicated. However, we will take a closer look at those fusions of actions where there are no radical switches in the flow. We are especially interested in how tactical conditions influence the linking of attacks and how we can thereby utilize our basic combinations.

Application of Combinations

With regard to the activity of our opponent, and relative to our own movements, we should use sequences of linked attacks in sports combat. We do not want the composition of these sequences to be left to coincidence. Consequently, we have deliberately selected six types of attacks with the foot, which we link with two types of hand attacks. As presented in the chapter on technical components, we achieve in this way 12 technical combinations which, if performed with the left and the right side, give us a total of 24 basic combinations. Their application in combat practice leads further to a practically unlimited number of variations. Both the composition and the implementation form of the applied combinations are determined by the following tactical circumstances:
- the preferred side and form of the initial fighting stance: left or right side stance, or, left or right reverse stance;
- distance and angle of attack: the use of tactical actions for adapting to changes of distance and position;
- the way in which the guarding arms of the opponent are neutralized, or deflected his/her attack upward or downward, inward or outward, only one or both hands, parallel or crossed, etc.;
- the height of the attacked vital point targeted by the foot or hand: head or torso;
- the execution distance for the attack: impact with a more or less extended attacking leg or arm.

Fig.115:
The sequence of fighting
in a sports bout

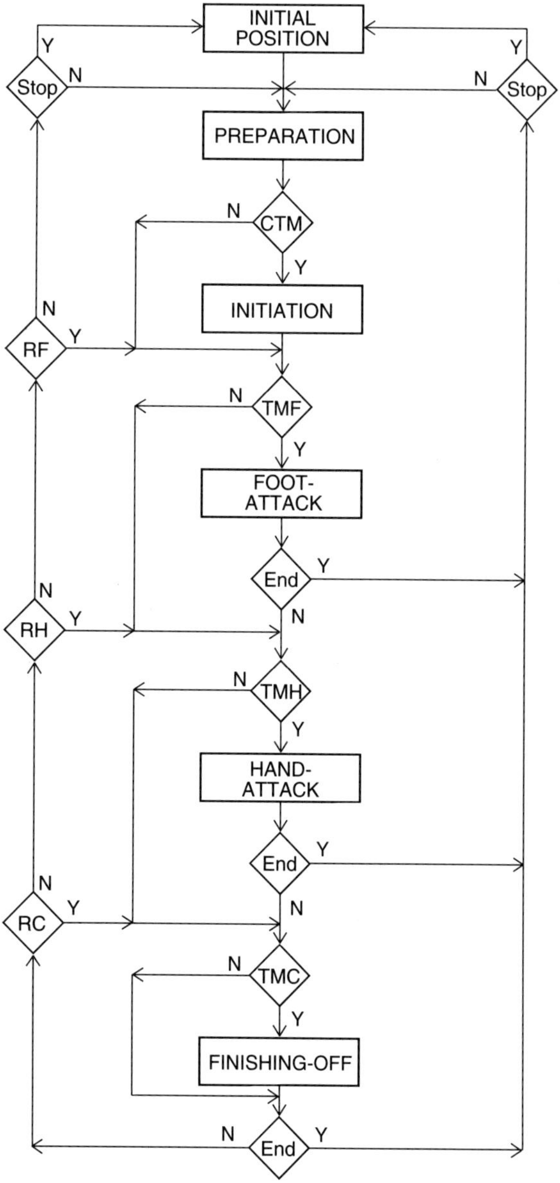

Legend:

CTM – Creation of a Tactical
Moment

TMF – Tactical Moment for
Foot attack

TMH – Tactical Moment for
Hand attack

TMC – Tactical Moment for
Conclusion
(finishing-off)

RF – Repeated Foot attack

RH – Repeated Hand attack

RC – Repeated Conclusion
(finishing-off)

End – Natural end of
engagement

Stop – Interruption of the
fighting by the referee

Y – Yes

N – No

Both – (a) variations of basic combinations, and (b) linking individual attacks with basic combinations, or several basic combinations together – we call *fighting combinations*. For clarity, we call (a) the first ones simply *'Combinations'* and (b) the second ones *'Series'*.

Fighting combinations are made up of mutually inter-linked movements, which an experienced fighter intuitively and automatically selects in response to circumstances in any given instant of combat. Certainly, we consider the circumstances, which occur often, to be types of tactical situations which we then systematically use for training in fighting combinations. Thus, we improve our capability to enact quick and suitable improvisations, when a given combat situation requires a particular reaction. Certain combinations or series, whether programmed or free-form, are especially suited to certain individuals and become eventually their specialty. There is a wide palette of possibilities available to any fighter for his/her personal selection within the framework of the fighting repertoire presented here. However, in spite of the great number of differences possible among all the various personal selections, our fighting repertoire does not lose its clarity nor its comprehensiveness.

In the next section we will illustrate the typical possibilities to vary combinations in attacks and counter-attacks. This is followed by an explanation of the composition of series and the significance of specialties. Additionally, we will clarify the characteristics and feasibility of jump attacks within the framework of our fighting repertoire.

BASIC FIGHTING VARIATIONS

Attack Variations

With an attack, we surprise or catch our opponent in a situation when he/she cannot decide whether to initiate an attack, or is even retreating. Several variations of attacks are possible, dependent on the appearance of the various tactical situations as they change. However, within the scope of this book, we will limit ourselves to the most typical ones. In order to simplify the comparison, we always start from a left fighting side stance, as we also always hit the opponent in the same stance.

We start with variations for the introductory attack, which depends mainly on the fighting distance to the opponent. This distance is measured differently, depending on the opponent's initial fighting stance:
- If the opponent takes a backward-leaning fighting stance *(kokutsu-dachi)*, the distance is measured from the lead foot of the attacker to the point on the ground under the opponent's center of gravity.
- If the opponent takes a forward-leaning fighting stance *(fudo-dachi)*, the distance is measured from the lead foot of the attacker to the lead foot of the opponent.

The unit of measure applied is not a normal unit of length, e.g., centimeters, but rather a personal, individual measure – steps. The length of a step varies with body height as well as with the length of each person's legs, and is thus always individual. This is, however, the only meaningful way of measuring any fighting distance: it is not important to know how many centimeters a certain fighting distance totals, but how an individual can bridge it when initiating an attack. Each fighter will always try to assume his/her particular, individual fighting distance, appropriate to his/her body size and to the length of his/her steps. The only hindrance to achieving this goal can be the body size and the preferred fighting distance of his/her opponent.

Regardless of the body size of a fighter, each type of attack has its particular, best striking distance. We call this distance the optimum striking distance, because at this distance, the corresponding attacks can be executed directly, without using preliminary distance bridging. However, there is no initiating action only when we attack with the rear foot. If we attack with the lead foot at the direct distance, we have first to introduce the attack by shifting the back foot to be beside the lead foot (shifting feet or leaping). When we attack from a fighting distance greater than a direct one, we need to bridge it by a shorter or longer left lunge or right step. Referring to Table 2 in the previous chapter, you will recall that every kind of foot attack has six typical introductions used for bridging three main fighting distances.

The optimum striking distance is identical to the action range of corresponding types of attacks (for now, we ignore the fact that the distances for a kick to the head and the same kick to the torso are not equal). By experiment, one can easily recognize that there are four groups of optimum striking distances (compare Table 3, p. 112):

- ◆ clinch or contact distance: for direct attacks with 5A and 6B onto both legs; also for half-extended short attacks with 1B and 2A as well as for finishing-off blocks and bars; the attacker's lead leg is as close as possible to the opponent, which means that this distance totals zero;
- ◆ close distance: for short direct attacks with 1B and 2A; for 5A and 6B onto front leg; for direct attacks with 11A and 12B; this distance is about half of a normal step longer than the clinch distance;
- ◆ short distance: for direct attacks with 3A and 4B, also 9A and 10B; this distance is about one normal step longer than the clinch distance (fig. 116, p. 113);
- ◆ medium distance: for direct attacks with 1A and 2B; this distance is about one attacking step longer than the clinch distance(fig. 117, p. 113).

Considering that each attack can be applied also at a greater distance than the optimum one, this gives two more fighting distances (compare table 3):

- ◆ long distance: with tactical introduction suitable for the type of attack I, II, and V; this distance is approximately two average steps longer than the clinch distance (fig. 118, p. 113);
- ◆ very long distance: suitable for properly introduced attacks of type I; this distance is two attack strides longer than the clinch distance (fig. 119, p. 113).

Table 3 (p. 112) gives an overview of the suitability of the typical fighting distances for the six types of attacks. It is obvious from the table, that the most universal one is the short distance, as it can be applied with various introductions of all types and kinds of attacks. The next most suitable is the medium distance. Both of the two shorter distances are rather risky and, in any event, are used mostly when they occur by themselves in the course of a bout. The two longer distances are rarely used as initial fighting distances, because they require long introductions, which enables the opponent to anticipate the following attack more easily.

This covers the interdependency of variations of attacks in the introductory phase. We can now move onto the next logical step – the implementation or execution phase of attack. The main variations of the 12 combinations in this phase are shown in figs. 120–167, pp. 114–125. Here, we consider all four forms of the six types of combinations – straight or reverse, left or right hand attack – which we use for the presentation of the following variations of attacks:

- ◆ Attacks with the leg
  - • high (to the head)
    - – with the upper part of the foot
    - – with the ball of the foot
    - – with the heel
    - – with the full sole of the foot
  - • medium (to the torso)
    - – with the upper part of the foot
    - – with the ball of the foot
    - – with the heel
    - – with the full sole of the foot
  - • low (onto the lower leg, standing)
    - – with the full sole of the foot
- ◆ Attacks with the hand
  - • fist punch
    - – with extended arm
      - ⋯ to the head
      - ⋯ to the torso
    - – with half-flexed arm
      - ⋯ to the head
      - ⋯ to the torso
  - • fist strike (to the head)
    - – with extended arm
    - – with half-flexed arm
- ◆ Deflections and blocks with all variations of hand attacks
  - • up-outward
  - • up-inward

How much the attacking arm has to be extended in order to reach the targeted vital point, depends on whether the defender has evaded the preceding foot attack by moving back, and by how much he/she has moved.

Each of the combinations presented in the main, attack execution phase (figs. 120–167, pp. 114–125), is only one of many variations. It could also look different in a sufficiently different fighting situation. The finishing-off actions are not presented for each combination separately. The details depend on the reaction of the opponent who we are trying to hold under control in a state of RAS. Variations of finishing-off are presented with a few examples in figures 168–177, p. 127.

Distance in long attack steps	Distance in regular steps	Type of attack	I				II				III				IV				V				VI			
		Combination	1		2		3		4		5		6		7		8		9		10		11		12	
		Attack with hand	A	B	A	B	A	B	A	B	A	B	A	B	A	B	A	B	A	B	A	B	A	B	A	B
		Attack with foot	R	L	L	R	R	L	L	R	R	L	L	R	R	L	L	R	R	L	L	R	R	L	L	R
	0	clinch distance		d)	d)						d)	n	n	d)												
	0,5	close distance		1)	1)						l	p	p	l	d	n	n	d					d	n	n	d
	1	short distance	d)	g)	g)	d)	d	n	n	d	g	s	s	g	l	p	p	l	d	n	n	d	l	p	p	l
1	1	medium distance	d	n	n	d	l	p	p	l					g	s	s	g	l	p	p	l	g	s	s	g
2	2	long distance	l	p	p	l	g	s	s	g									g	s	s	g				
2	2	very long distance	g	s	s	g																				

Table 3: Introduction of attacks in relation to the fighting distance

Legend:

d – *direct execution (optimal striking distance)*

n – *shifting back foot to the fore (optimum striking distance)*

l – *introduced with lunge*

p – *introduced with pre-jump*

g – *introduced with spring (longer lunge)*

s – *introduced with stride (long step)*

) – *short variations of type I attacks*

The attacker is standing in the left fighting side stance. The reference distance is the clinch distance, i.e., the distance of a half extended arm just hitting one of the vital points of the opponent, in steps total zero. The table shows that the only fighting distance, from which all types and kinds of attacks (direct or introduced) are possible, is the short fighting distance. It is also the most commonly applied in practice. The next most common one is the medium fighting distance.

116
*Short fighting distance:
This is an average step
longer than the clinch
distance. Suitable for all
types and kinds of attacks.*

Fig. 116–119:
Some
fighting
distances

117
*Medium fighting distance:
This is an attack step
longer than the clinch
distance. The second most
suitable fighting distance.*

118
*Long fighting distance:
This is two average steps
longer than the clinch
distance.*

119
*Very long fighting distance:
This is two attack steps
longer than the clinch
distance.*

113

Fig. 120–127: Attacks of type I

Combination 1A   *Combination 2A*

120   122

121   123

To fig. 120: The attack with a step is almost finished. Establishing control of the opponent's protective arm with A-up-in interception, the right hand is bending for a punch ...

To fig. 121: ... and in the next moment, shortly before the striking foot touches down, the attacker punches with his fist to the opponent's torso under the up-in (sukui-uchi) deflected hand. The finishing-off follows.

To fig. 122: Before the end of the attacking step forward, we create an opening by intercepting using an up-out against the opponent's guarding arm and simultaneously bending for the right fist punch.

To fig. 123: The touchdown of the left foot follows, preceded by an up-out deflection (sukui-soto) of the opponent's guarding arm to the side. At the same time, we throw a reverse punch with the right hand (gyaku-tsuki) to the opponent's head. Here, the climax of the punch is already over, and, as obvious from the high position of the heel, the right leg has already started moving into the finishing-off position.

Combination 1B	Combination 2B
124	126

| 125 | 127 |

To fig. 124: Before the end of the long step forward, we gain control over the opponent's guarding arm with an up-out deflection, while the left shoulder and arm are bending for a straight fist punch.

To fig. 125: While the right hand is controlling the opponent's protecting arm, the opponent's head has been hit by a left punch, the lead foot touching down immediately thereafter.

To fig. 126: Before completing the step with the right foot, we gain control over the opponent's guarding arm with A-up-out, and bend simultaneously the left shoulder and arm for the reverse fist punch to follow.

To fig. 127: Before touching down the striking foot, we executed a reverse fist punch into the torso (gyaku-tsuki), thereby keeping control over the opponent's lead arm. The left foot has already started its movement forward into the final position, and the finishing-off follows.

115

Fig. 128–135: Attacks of type II

Combination 3A   *Combination 4A*

128   130

129   131

To fig. 128: Right front kick – reverse thrust with the foot R3 (gyaku-mae-geri) to the stomach; the opponent is retreating just ...

To fig. 129: ... to the right distance for our straight fist punch (oi-tsuki) to the head.. This is executed over the opponent's guarding arm with a B-up-in (sukui-uchi) sideways and down, the striking foot touching down immediately afterwards.

To fig. 130: Left front kick – straight thrust with the foot L4 (oi-mae-geri). Opponent is struck in the stomach while sliding backward ...

To fig. 131: ... and this is immediately followed up by a reverse right fist punch (gyaku-tsuki) to the torso and under the opponent's guarding arm, controlled by B-up-in.

Combination 3B

Combination 4B

132

134

133

135

To fig. 132: Pretended attack with a left front reverse kick (gyaku-mae-geri) to the head – high thrust with the foot L3; the opponent is outside the range, so all we can indeed do, is to gain control over his guarding hand.

To fig. 133: Because the opponent has not retreated, we are able to reach him with a straight fist punch (oi-tsuki) passing the guarding arm which has been deflected with the A-up-out (sukui-soto).

To fig. 134: The opponent is again outside our reach, and, consequently, our right straight high kick (oi-mae-geri) – a thrust with the right foot R4 to the head – is a feinted attack only. The opponent is attempting a retreat ...

To fig. 135: ... but we still reach him with a long reverse fist punch B2 (gyaku-tsuki) to the stomach, after we have gained and kept control over the opponent's guarding arm with an A-up-out (sukui-soto). We are in a long reverse attacking stance, with the heel lifted up to the maximum as the foot has just started shifting into its final position. The finishing-off follows.

Fig. 136–143: Attacks of type III

Combination 5A

136

Combination 6B

138

137

139

To fig. 136: Sweep with the right leg R5 (ashi-barai) of the opponent's front leg to disturb his balance, while we also gain control over his guarding hand. The opponent has transferred his body weight onto the standing leg just in time and will, therefore, not fall down but will be spun away to the side.

To fig. 137: With this, however, his whole left side remains unguarded. We adjust to the new axis and throw a straight right fist-punch A1 (oi-tsuki) to the head, and at the same time control his guarding hand with a B-up-out.

To fig. 138: Clinch or contact striking distance. After having gained control of the opponent's guarding arm with the B-up-out, we drive our right arm across his chest all the way through to his right shoulder, and push him sideways downwards. Simultaneously, we hook his front leg with a right sickle-like hook R6 and pull through ...

To fig. 139: ... so that the opponent falls down. While adapting our position to the new attack axis, and changing our posture correspondingly, as well as re-establishing control – if necessary – over the opponent's guarding hand with an up-in (sukui-uchi), we attack him with a reverse left fist punch B2 (gyaku-tsuki). The finishing-off follows.

Sweeping or hooking the opponent's front lower leg from the inside outward – as would be the case when applying combinations 5B and 6A on an opponent standing in a left stance (left lead leg) – can have rather adverse results, as we can easily injure the opponent's shin (as well as our own) or his/her knee when he/she falls down. For that reason we show here, instead, variations of 5A and 6B attacking both legs.

140

142

141

143

To fig. 140: Before the attack, we step alongside the opponent's front foot - that is at a clinch or contact distance - removing the opponent's guarding hand with a right up-in deflection and putting the left hand on his right shoulder. We then sweep both of the opponent's legs away, simultaneously exerting pressure on his right shoulder in the direction opposite to the sweep-attack.

To fig. 141: While the opponent was falling down, we adapted our posture to the new situation, as well as gained control over the opponent's guarding arm (here with a B-up-out), and delivered a straight right fist punch A1 (oi-tsuki). The finishing-off follows.

To fig. 142: Using the same preliminary actions, with the arms as in an attack on the front leg only (cf. fig. 138), we now attack both legs. The leading right hand is helping here as well by pushing the right shoulder of the opponent in the direction opposite to the sweep, diagonally downward.

To fig. 143: The opponent is on the ground. While he was falling, we adjusted the attack axis and adapted our body posture to the new situation. We also kept control – as much as necessary – over the opponent's guarding arm and followed him with a left reverse fist punch B2 (gyaku-tsuki).

Fig. 144–151: Attacks of type IV

Combination 7A

144

145

Combination 8A

146

147

To fig. 144: Front reverse roundhouse kick R7 (gyaku-mawashi-geri) with the instep of the right foot to the opponent's ribs. The opponent tried to evade it, but was "caught". We control his guarding arm with a B-up-out (sukui-soto)

To fig. 145: A short punch, or hammer-like strike, with A1 (oi-tetsui-tsuki) to the head followed.

To fig. 146: Front straight roundhouse kick L8 (oi-mawashi-geri) with the instep of the left foot to the head. The opponent is trying a sideways evasion with his head.

To fig. 147: After gaining control over of his/her guarding arm with a B-up-in (sukui-uchi), we execute the right fist punch A2 (gyaku-tsuki) to the torso, with a halfway extended arm due to the given distance.

Combination 7B

148

Combination 8B

150

149

To fig. 148: Front reverse roundhouse kick (gyaku-mawashi-geri) L7 with the instep of the left foot to the head. The guarding arm is controlled with an A-up-out (sukui-soto). The opponent is not retreating.

To fig. 149: We now remove his protection with a simultaneous short straight fist punch with the left hand to the torso B1 (oi-tsuki).

151

To fig. 150: Front straight roundhouse kick (oi-mawashi-geri) R8 with the ball of the right foot to the torso. The leading hand has caught his guarding arm with an A-up-in (sukui-uchi). The opponent has transferred his weight onto the rear leg thus moving also slightly backwards.

To fig. 151: Keeping control over the opponent's guard, we deliver a reverse fist punch B2 (gyaku-tsuki) thereby extending our left arm fully, as the striking distance requires it.

Fig. 152–159: Attacks of type V

Combination 9A	*Combination 10A*
152	154

153

155

To fig. 152: After the introductory turn, we follow with a back (reverse) thrust kick R9 (ushiro-geri) with the heel to the torso.

To fig. 153: After the strike - during the pulling back of the striking foot and the upwards swinging and turning of the thigh – the left hand has introduced and led the turning of the body further until it has gained control over the opponent's guarding arm with an up-in (sukui-uchi). At the same time, the opponent has slightly retreated. A straight right fist punch A1 (oi-tsuki) has just hit the opponent's head.

To fig. 154: After turning the hips, and taking one introductory step in the direction of the opponent, we execute a backward (straight) side kick (ushiro-yoko-geri) with the left heel to the torso. The left lead hand is at the same time controlling the opponent's guarding hand with a B-up-out (sukui-soto).

To fig. 155: After rechambering the striking leg, we straighten the body, and twist the heel of the right foot outwards, so that the shoulders and arms are bent ready for the right reverse fist-punch A2 (gyaku-tsuki) – which we are now executing. Beforehand, we changed the controlling hand to an up-in and so created a corridor for our punch.

Combination 9B

156

Combination 10B

158

157

159

To fig. 156: Back (reverse) thrust kick L9 (ushiro-geri) with the left heel to the head.

To fig. 157: During the rechambering of the striking foot, and the straightening of the body, the right arm continues to induce the turning of the body until it has gained control over the opponent's guarding arm with an up-in (sukui-uchi). At the same time, the left arm has been bent for a fist punch B1 (oitsuki) to the torso – which we have just executed.

To fig. 158: Backward (straight) side kick R10 (yoko-ushiro-geri) with the right heel to the head. The opponent has leaned back and evaded the kick, which has thus become equal to a pretended one.

To fig. 159: After we have reverted the hips, rechambered the striking foot, and straightened up the body, we bend the left shoulder and arm for a reverse fist punch B2 (gyakutsuki) to the torso, and have just executed it while controlling the opponent's guarding hand with an A-up-out (sukui-soto). The finishing-off follows.

123

Fig. 160–167: Attacks of type VI

Combination 11A

160

Combinatuon 12A

162

161

163

To fig. 160: After the introductory turn, we execute a back (reverse) roundhouse kick R11(ushiro-mawashi-geri) with the right heel to the torso.

To fig. 161: During the rechambering of the kicking leg and straightening up the body, the left arm continues to turn the body, pushing all the way through until it has gained control over the opponent's guarding hand with an up-in (sukui-uchi). The right side of the body is bent and we execute the right straight fist punch A1 (oi-tsuki) past the controlled arm. Because of the preceding kick, the opponent has moved slightly and bends backwards, thus moving into the optimum striking distance.

To fig. 162: After turning the hips and taking one introductory step towards the opponent, we are now executing a back reverted (straight) roundhouse kick L12 (mostly called "reverse" roundhouse kick, ura-mawashi-geri) with the left foot to the head. The leading hand is controlling the opponent's guarding arm with an up-out (sukui-soto).

To fig. 163: After we have reverted the hips, rechambered the lower leg, straightened up the body, and twisted the right heel outwards, we bend the shoulders and execute the right reverse fist punch A2 (gyaku-tsuki). Since the opponent has not retreated much, we have performed the punch with a slightly flexed arm.

Combination 11B   Combination 12B

164   166

165   167

To fig. 164: Back (reverse) roundhouse kick L11 (ushiro-mawashi-geri) with the left heel or sole to the head.

To fig. 165: While the lower leg rechambers and the body straightens up, the right hand continues to induce the turn until control is gained over the opponent's guarding arm with an up-in (sukui-uchi), and the bending of the right arm. While the opponent slides slightly backwards, the left straight fist punch B1 (oi-tsuki) to the torso has been executed.

To fig. 166: Back reverted (straight) round-house kick (otherwise known mostly as "re-verse" roundhouse kick; ura-mawashi-geri) with the right foot to the torso. At the same time, the right arm has been controlling the opponent's guarding arm with an up-out (sukui-soto).

To fig. 167: While rechambering the strik-ing foot and straightening up the body, as well as twisting the heel of the support foot outwards, we bend and execute the left reverse fist punch B2 (gyaku-tsuki) to the head past the controlled arm. As the oppo-nent has remained at the same spot after the kick, the hand striking distance is suitable for a punch with a halfway flexed arm.

Counter-attack Variations

A counter-attack is an attack on the opponent at the moment when he/she is attacking us. Because the opponent him-/herself is bridging the distance between us and him/her, thus coming within his/her optimum striking distance, we do not need to carry out any distance bridging preliminary actions. We usually execute counter-attacks in three tactical variations:

- ◆ direct, intercepting counter-attack along the fighting axis, that is, on the same axis as the attack, but in the opposite direction;
- ◆ counter-attack from the side, after evasion to the left or right of the fighting axis;
- ◆ counter-attack after retreat backward.

We should disregard the third possibility above, because it is rather risky. This is – by moving backward, we indeed do evade the first attack, but thereafter find it difficult to initiate an attack forward. Also, the opponent can successfully exploit our retreat with a second or even further attack. At the very least, what we lose, by retreating backward, is the initiative to actively conduct combat. In principle, we consider a retreat backwards as the last resort for saving ourselves from an unfavorable situation. We do not need to learn this since everybody knows more or less instinctively how to do it. The other two possibilities, however, are very useful, so we will have a closer look at them.

Direct Counter-attacks

For a direct counter-attack, it is important that, as we start, the opponent is moving into the optimum striking distance for the kind of counter-attack we are carrying out. The direct counter-attack utilizes the state of RAS in which the opponent is most of the time during his/her attack. The best opportunity for this being the time interval of the technical introduction, i.e., between the start and the launching of the attack.

A successful direct counter-attack literally stops the opponent's forward movement (see figs 179–180, p. 129). The best counter-attacks are with the type I, II, and V, and in particular variations, also IV. Counter-attack types II and V run in the same way as the attacks at the direct distance. Counter-attack type I varies, however, as shown in the figures 181–184, p. 129, when the opponent attacks with a technically clean attack 1A.

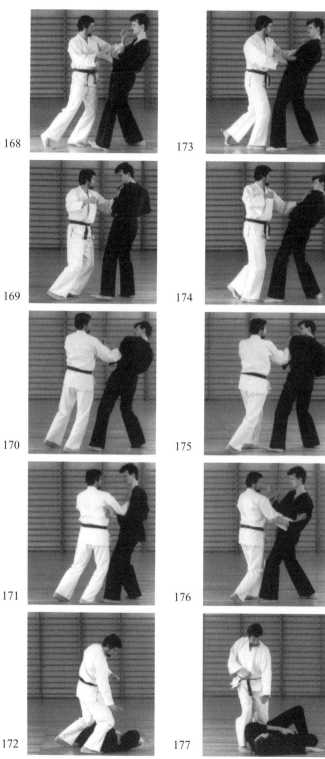

Fig.168–177:
Examples of
finishing-off
in a clinch

168
169
170
171
172
173
174
175
176
177

Short versions of attacks 2A and 1B, starting from a left fighting stance, are the fastest of all fighting combinations, and thus the most suitable for direct counter-attacks. They are executed purely with a whiplash motion of the attacking shoulder and arm, twisting or unwinding the torso, and transferring the body weight forward. Here we perform a lunge as a part of the counter-attack and it does not serve as a tactical introduction, as in the attack.

If our counter-attack is too late, we first have to deflect our opponent's attack. In this case, there is neither time, space, nor opportunity to make a lunge, and we therefore omit this part of the counter-attack (figs. 181–184, p. 129).

Side Counter-attacks

In a counter-attack, the time interval from the evasion to the side, away from the attack axis, which begins simultaneously with the launching of the opponent's attack, is utilized as the introduction phase. The opponent's attack consequently comes to nothing. Such an evasion means a change of position, with or without a change of stance. It is similar to the introductory bridging of the distance for an attack. However, here, we move sideways to establish an angle to the axis of the opponent's attack, and thus create a new axis for the counter-attack to follow. We execute it in a way similar to the preliminary tactical move forward, i.e., normally with one or two shiftings of the feet, but in this case stepping aside and usually also backward, instead.

The evasion to the side and backwards influences the kind of combination used in a counter-attack, especially the foot attacks. Here, various differences between individuals become obvious, especially with regard to their motor adaptability and personal preferences for certain attacks. But more importantly, the difference is made by stepping aside with just one shift of the foot (1 SF), or with two shifts of the feet (2 SF). Making only one side-step, that is only one shift of foot, is of course shorter and therefore usually faster. However, when attacking after just one side-step, we usually cannot execute all of the foot attacks equally well and smoothly. Some of them lose so much force and smoothness that it is significantly better to perform them after an introduction with two side-steps. However, because we cannot choose the timing of the opponent's attack, and thus cannot know which leg our weight will be on when we have to begin our evasion, we just have to master both variations; the one with one side-step and the one with two side-steps.

Table 4 (p. 130) gives an overview of the suitability of the 12 combinations in the counter-attack after an evasion to the side of the fighting axis. This overview may serve only as a basic guideline, because substantial individual deviations from the average are possible.

To fig. 179–180: Counter-attack with B1 (oi-tsuki) and 2A (gyaku tsuki), accomplished with a lunge. The start of the counter-attack is executed almost simultaneously with the start of the opponent's attack. This is only possible, however, when we are able to read his intentions in time. With this counter-attack, we literally stop the opponent. This works best if we catch him when he has transferred all his weight onto the front (standing) leg, and his striking foot or hand has not yet reached the launching position – this is, so to speak, during the initiation of the attack. During the counter-attack, the free hand is in a guarding position, just in case we are too late and have to prevent an already launched attack.

179   180

181   182

Figures 179–184:
Direct counter-attack type I

To fig. 181–184: Counter-attacks 1B (oi-tsuki) and 2A (gyaku-tsuki), performed with a deflection in case we are too late for the direct variation. The following examples of deflections with simultaneous punches are shown here: up-out (sukui-age soto; fig. 181, 184) and up-in (sukui-age-uchi; fig. 182, 183); with accompanying hand punch 2A (gyaku-tsuki; fig. 181, 183) and 1B (oi-tsuki; fig. 182, 184). If the opponent attacked our torso, we would use the deflections down-out (sukui-otoshi-soto) and down-in (sukui-otoshi-uchi).

183   184

129

In the following pages, we will present the main phases of introduction – with one or two side-steps – and the execution of counter-attacks with the foot in each of the twelve combinations. Counter-attacks with the hand are presented only for variations of type I attacks. Otherwise we assume that the hand attacks in all the combinations are well known, especially because the preliminary side-steps do not influence hand attacks very much.

Counter-attacks from the side are successful under the following conditions:
- The opponent has first to bridge some distance before getting in position to launch his/her attack; because of this, his/her intention becomes visible early enough and the defender, anticipating the kind of attack, has enough time to prepare the evasion and the proper counter-attack.
- The defender begins the evasion at the right time, that is:
  - not too early, when the attacker could still adapt the attack to a new angle; if this happens, the defender will find him-/herself practically in a direct counter-attack;
  - not too late, when it becomes impossible to prevent the opponent's attack with a deflection. In such a case, the sidewards evasion loses its original meaning and becomes more a support to the deflection.

Table 4: Basic combinations in the counter-attack from the side: usefulness of variations with one side-step (1 SF)

Type of attack		I				II				III				IV				V				VI			
Combination	Straight	1				3				5				7				9				11			
	Reverse			2				4				6				8				10				12	
	Hand attack	A	B	A	B	A	B	A	B	A	B	A	B	A	B	A	B	A	B	A	B	A	B	A	B
	Foot attack	R	L	L	R	R	L	L	R	R	L	L	R	R	L	L	R	R	L	L	R	R	L	L	R
Eva-sion	To the left	+	+	+	+	+	0	0	+	X	0	0	X	+	?	?	+	?	0	+	+	?	0	+	+
	To the right	+	+	+	+	+	?	?	+	+	X	X	+	+	?	?	+	+	0	+	?	+	0	+	?

Legend:

+	–	*favorable (preferable to the variation with two sidesteps, i.e., 2 SF)*
?	–	*partially favorable (depending on the situation and motoric ability of the performer, possibly faster than 2 SF).*
0	–	*unfavorable (technically possible, but in most cases the variation with 2 SF is more favorable)*
X	–	*useless (tactically, though technically possible)*

The counter-attack has been started from the left fighting side stance.

- The attacker has misjudged the defender's readiness to start; he/she wrongly assumes the defender is in, or is getting into a state of RAS, thus being incapable of starting a counter-attack.
- The defender is utilizing the kind of counter-attack which is a proper response to the given attack, i.e., targeting the exposed vital points.

We will not continue to discuss, at this point, how to fulfill all these conditions. That would require a lot more space than it is available in this book. Here we will present, with illustrations and comments, only the technical adaptation of basic combinations to certain tactical situations, without trying to demonstrate all the tactical factors. For simplicity of presentation, we imagine the same as with a direct counter-attack: the opponent attacks with a technically clean 1A to the head, to which the defender responds with all the combinations in turn (figs .185–260).

Early forms of European karate-like fighting

One of the drawings from the book Der künstliche Ringer (The Skilled Fighter), by N. Petter, written 1674. The attacker is applying a straight, direct fist-punch.

131

189   190   191   192   193

Fig. 185–193:
Counter-attacks with the RIGHT
foot after evasion to the LEFT:
STRAIGHT combinations

185

To fig. 185:
Introduction with 1 SF.
Evasion to the left of the
fighting axis with the left
foot. This provides a push-
off point and launching
point in accordance with
the kind of counter-attack
to follow: suitable for most
attacks, partially favo-
rable for R9 and R11, use-
less for R5.

187   186   188

To fig. 186–188: Introduction with 2 SF.
Evasion to the left of the fighting axis, first with the right foot
(fig. 186); from this new position, we start a selected counter-
attack simultaneously shifting the left foot onto a new push-
off point, as required by the kind of attack just started: in fig.
187 we are just introducing one of the counter-attacks
forward, while fig. 188 shows the introduction into one of the
backward kicks

| 198 | 199 | 200 | 201 | 202 |

Fig. 194–202:
Counter-attacks with the RIGHT
foot after evasion to the LEFT:
REVERSE combinations

194

To fig. 194:
Introduction with 1 SF.
The right foot starts an
attack while we are
still shifting the left
foot to the left of the
fighting axis and onto
its new push-off point
suitable for the kind of
counter-attack star-
ted; useless for R6.

| 196 | 195 | 197 |

To fig. 195–197: Introduction with 2 SF.
First we shift the right foot into a new starting position left
of the fighting axis (fig. 195), and start an attack immediately afterwards; simultaneously with the start, we shift the
left foot onto its new push-off point that suits the kind of
counter-attack we are implementing. In fig. 196, we have
just started one of the counter-attacks forward, and in
fig.197, we are introducing one of the backward kicks.

133

To fig. 203:
Introduction with 1 SF.
We have just shifted the
right foot onto its new
push-off point to the left
of the fighting axis, se-
lected according to the
kind of counter-attack
to follow. Immediately
afterwards, we start a
counter-attack with the
left lead leg; partially
suitable for L7, L3, L5,
unsuitable for L9 and
L11.

Fig. 203–212:
Counter-attacks with the LEFT
foot after evasion to the LEFT:
STRAIGHT combinations

205   204   206

To fig. 204–206: Introduction with 2 SF.
First, we move our left foot onto a new starting point to the
left and slightly rearwards relative to the previous one (fig.
204), and start a selected attack. Meanwhile, we are shift-
ing the right foot onto its new push-off point that suits the
kind of counter-attack just started: in fig. 205 this is shown
for an attack forward, and in fig. 206 for a backward kick.

203

207   208   209   210   211   212

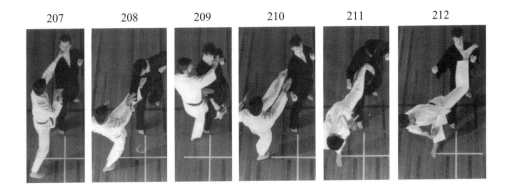

Fig. 213–222:
Counter-attacks with the LEFT
foot after evasion to the LEFT:
REVERSE combinations

*To fig. 213:
Introduction with 1 SF.
We shift the right foot
onto a new push-off
point left of the fight-
ing axis, while we start
a counter-attack with
the left foot; partially
suitable for L4, L6, and
L8.*

213

215   214   216

*To fig. 214–216: Introduction with 2 SF.
First, we shift the left foot slightly backward and to the
left of the fighting axis onto a new starting point (fig.
214). Then, we start immediately, while at the same
time shifting the right foot onto a new push-off point as
necessary for the kind of counter-attack just started: in
fig. 215 this is shown for a counter-attack forward,
and in fig. 216 for a kick backward.*

217   218   219   220   221   222

| 231 | 230 | 229 | 228 | 227 |

Fig. 223–231:
Counter-attacks with the LEFT
foot after evasion to the RIGHT:
STRAIGHT combinations

225   224   226

To fig. 224–226: Introduction with 2 SF.
First, we shift the left foot slightly backwards and to the
right of the fighting axis onto a new starting point (fig.
224), and, while starting, the right foot is moved onto a
new push-off point chosen in accordance with the kind
of attack started: in fig. 225 shown for counter-attacks
forward and in fig. 226 for backward kicks.

223

To fig. 223:
Introduction with 1 SF.
We shift the right foot to the
right of the fighting axis
onto a new push-off point
that is suitable for the kind
of counter-attack to follow;
simultaneously, we start a
counter-attack with the left
lead foot: partially suitable
for L3 and L7, unsuitable
for L9 and L11, useless for
L5.

| 240 | 239 | 238 | 237 | 236 |

Fig. 232–240:
Counter-attacks with the LEFT
foot after evasion to the RIGHT:
REVERSE combinations

232

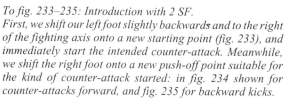

234   233   235

To fig. 233–235: Introduction with 2 SF.
First, we shift our left foot slightly backwards and to the right
of the fighting axis onto a new starting point (fig. 233), and
immediately start the intended counter-attack. Meanwhile,
we shift the right foot onto a new push-off point suitable for
the kind of counter-attack started: in fig. 234 shown for
counter-attacks forward, and fig. 235 for backward kicks.

To fig. 232:
Introduction with 1
SF.
While the right foot
is shifted onto a new
push-off point to the
right of the fighting
axis – suitable for the
kind of counter-at-
tack to follow – we
start the chosen kick
with the left foot:
partially suitable for
L4 and L8, useless
for L6.

137

Fig. 241–250:
Counter-attacks with the RIGHT
foot after evasion to the RIGHT:
STRAIGHT combinations

To fig. 241:
Introductions with 1 SF
The right foot starts a
selected counter-attack
while we are shifting the
left foot onto a new push-
off point to the right of
the fighting axis,
suitable for the kind of
counter-attack we are
just implementing; suit-
able for all kinds of at-
tack.

241

244 242 243

To fig. 242–244: Introduction with 2 SF.
We shift the right foot slightly backward and to the right
of the fighting axis onto a new starting point (fig. 242),
and immediately start the intended counter-attack.
Meanwhile, we shift the left foot onto a new push-off
point suitable for the kind of attack just started: in fig.
243 shown for counter-attacks forward, and in fig. 244
for backward kicks.

250 249 248 247 246 245

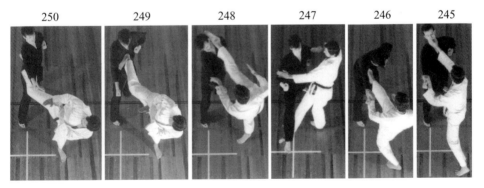

Fig. 251–260:
Counter-attacks with the RIGHT
foot after evasion to the RIGHT:
REVERSE combinations

To fig. 251:
Introduction with 1 SF.
The right foot starts a selected
counter-attack, while we are
shifting the left foot onto its
new push-off point to the right
of the fighting axis as required
by the kind of counter-attack
started; suitable for all kinds
of attacks, but only partially
for R10 and R12.

251

| 254 | 252 | 253 |

To fig. 252–254:Introduction with 2 SF.
First, we shift our right foot slightly backward and to
the right of the fighting axis onto a new starting point
(fig. 252), and immediately start a counter-attack.
Meanwhile, we are shifting the left foot onto its new
push-off point, as necessary for the attack just started:
in fig. 253 shown for counter-attacks forward, and in
fig. 254 for backward kicks.

| 260 | 259 | 258 | 257 | 256 | 255 |

Fig. 261: Model for the composition of series

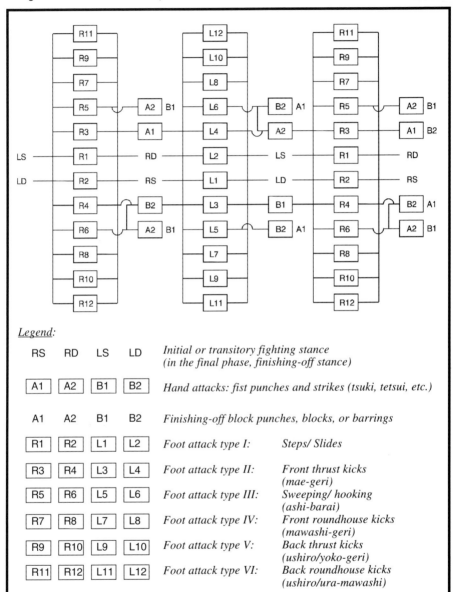

Legend:

RS RD LS LD				*Initial or transitory fighting stance (in the final phase, finishing-off stance)*
A1 A2 B1 B2				*Hand attacks: fist punches and strikes (tsuki, tetsui, etc.)*
A1 A2 B1 B2				*Finishing-off block punches, blocks, or barrings*
R1 R2 L1 L2				*Foot attack type I:* *Steps/ Slides*
R3 R4 L3 L4				*Foot attack type II:* *Front thrust kicks (mae-geri)*
R5 R6 L5 L6				*Foot attack type III:* *Sweeping/ hooking (ashi-barai)*
R7 R8 L7 L8				*Foot attack type IV:* *Front roundhouse kicks (mawashi-geri)*
R9 R10 L9 L10				*Foot attack type V:* *Back thrust kicks (ushiro/yoko-geri)*
R11 R12 L11 L12				*Foot attack type VI:* *Back roundhouse kicks (ushiro/ura-mawashi)*

Note: The flowchart above must be read from left to right and vertically only!

FREE FIGHTING VARIATIONS

A contestant's mastery of the sports fighting repertoire only becomes apparent when he/she can freely combine and vary his/her fighting actions according to current fighting situations. Only upon reaching this level can we begin to talk about being actually ready for fighting.

Series

In the same way that the basic combinations are put together, we can also link each of the basic combinations with various initiations, transitions, individual attacks, or even with another basic combination. The relevant factors to consider are the current fighting circumstances as well as the kinetic relativity of the inter-linked actions.

As to the fighting circumstances, continuing with further attacks becomes meaningful only when the opponent has managed to evade, block off, or deflect the first attack, or, the first attack has just been used as a feint or as a threat to get the opponent moving.

From a human kinetic point of view, certain attacks are more difficult to combine than others. For example attack 9 or 11 is more difficult to begin immediately after a punch has been thrown. We observe with many attacks that they are easier to link on one side, and at certain angles, than on the other side (see figure 262, p. 143).

Considering here again our basic kinetic scheme, freely-composed combinations can have two, three, or more phases (steps, or suppressed steps), whereby we link individual attacks, basic combinations, or both, with or without initiating actions in between (which thus become transitory actions). In extreme cases, we can combine only foot or only hand attacks. There can also be only one foot attack applied – in certain situation – followed immediately by a finishing-off block.

Correctly composed free combinations are called 'series'. Figure 261 (p. 140) presents a model for the formation of series which shows all possible linking of attacks into three up to seven-phased combinations. More than three attacks in a row

row are, however, rarely used in sports fighting, but we want to show here that this is, at least theoretically, not a limit.

Figures 263–315 shows some examples of series which are composed from one individual attack and one basic combination.

Series are here designated with symbols for the first, individual attack and the following combination, for example, series R5+8A. Our figures show only the first and the second attack. The rest, we assume, are already known and therefore unnecessary to repeat each time anew. For a better comparison, the attacker always begins from a left sid- stance and attacks first with the right foot and after that with the left foot.

Early forms of European karate-like fighting

From a book by J. Happel, Das Freifechten *(Free-Fighting), written in 1865. Fighting combinations, similar to those in karate, have been known in Europe and described long before the first book on karate was published in Japan in 1922. It is really amazing that the author has already clearly discerned between a reverse or diametrical kick (above) and a straight or same-sided kick (below), though he did not call them these names. This differentiation, important especially for grasping and learning various possibilities of the hand strikes to follow, has not been recognized in traditional karate yet, despite being applied in sports competitions.*

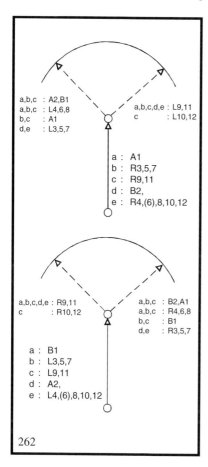

263

264

265

Fig. 262:
Further suitable attacks against an evading opponent

The diagram shows which kind of attacks fit kinetically best for further attacks when the opponent has evaded the first attack backward and away from the fighting axis in an attempt to initiate a counter-attack from the side.

To fig. 263–256: Series B1+6B

Instead of a finishing-off after a pretend attack with a B1 (fig. 263) to the head, we initiate the combination 6B (fig. 264) and hook the opponent's front leg away (fig. 265). A punch and a finishing-off block follows, (which we leave out here and in all following figures). If sweeping does not succeed, and the opponent is about to escape, then we could follow him with 2B, 4B, 8B, 10B, or 12B.

143

266

267

268

269

270

271

To fig. 266–268: Series A2+5A

After an ostensible attack A2 (fig. 266), we continue with combination 5A (fig. 267) and sweep the opponent's front leg away (fig. 268). If this is not successful and the opponent manages to escape, then we could follow up with 1A, 3A, 7A, 9A, or 11A.

To fig. 269–271: Series R3+6A

During an attack with a kick R3 (fig. 269), the opponent escapes with a step backward. With a suitable placing of the landing (striking) foot, we can immediately continue on to attack with 6A (fig. 270) and hook/sweep the opponent's front leg away (fig. 271).

272

274

273

275

To fig. 269, 272–273: Series R3+4A

While the opponent is escaping after R3, we put the striking foot down in such a way that we can continue with combination 4A (fig. 272) and execute a straight thrust kick 4 (fig. 273). Similarly, we could follow with 2A or 8A.

To fig. 269, 274–275: Series R3+10A

After attack R3 and the opponent's retreat, we start with combination 10A (fig. 274) and perform a left back (straight) side kick 10 (fig. 275). Similarly, we could also follow with 12A.

276

277

278

To fig. 276–278: Series L4–5A

The opponent is escaping during our thrust kick L4 (fig. 276), yet we still reach him/her with combination 5A (fig. 277), sweeping away both legs this time (fig. 278).

279

280

281

282

To fig. 276, 279–280: Series L4+3A

After an attack with L4, we follow the escaping opponent with combination 3A (fig. 279) performing a reverse-thrust kick 3 (fig. 280). Similarly, we could also apply 1A or 7A.

To fig. 276, 281–182: Series L4+9A

After an attack with L4, we turn during the landing and start again with combination 9A (fig. 281). We perform a back-(reverse) thrust kick 9 (fig. 282). Similarly, we could also apply 11A.

283

284

286

285

287

To fig. 283–285: Series R5+8A

Sweeping away the opponent's lead leg with R5 is partially successful (fig. 283) and has spun the opponent away from the fighting axis. We start with combination 8A (fig. 284) and perform a left front straight roundhouse kick 8 to the torso (fig. 285).

To fig. 283, 286–287: Series R5+11B

After sweeping, we start to turn for combination 11B (fig. 286) and execute a back (reverse) roundhouse kick 11 (fig. 287) to the head with a variation, in which the same hand, that is about to perform the hand attack, is now controlling the opponent's guard. The kick could also be directed to the torso, or, we could also use combination 9A.

288

289

291

290

292

To fig. 288–290: Series R7+8A

An ostensible attack with kick R7 to the head the opponent is escaping (fig. 288). The striking foot is landing so that the fighting axis has slightly shifted and we start with combination 8A (fig. 289), performing a left front straight roundhouse kick 8 to the head (fig. 290). Similarly we could also use 2A, 4A, or 6A.

To fig. 288, 291–292: Series R7+9B

After a high kick R7, which the opponent evades with a backward movement, we land with the striking foot in a back stance and with the leg in a launching position (fig. 291) ready for combination 9B. It follows the left back (reverse) thrust kick L9 to the torso (fig. 292), with the opposite hand in a protective position. In the same way we could also perform combination 11B.

293

294

296

295

297

To fig. 293–295: Series L8+7A

During a high kick L8 the opponent has evaded this in a backward direction (fig. 293). The striking foot lands slightly to the right of the fighting axis (fig. 294). We then start the combination 7A, attacking with a high right front reverse round-house kick 7 (fig. 295) past the opponent's guarding arm, which we control with our left hand. We could also use combinations 5A, 3A or 1A.

To fig. 293, 296–297: Series L8+11A

During the touch down of the striking foot after L8, we turn and start with combination 11A (fig. 296), executing now a high right back (reverse) round-house kick. Here we control the opponent's guard, using the hand to punch in the follow-up attack (fig. 297). We could also use combination 9A.

298

299

300

301

302

To fig. 298–300: Series R9+10A

To fig. 298, 301–302: Series R9+8A

An attack with a back (reverse) thrust kick R9 – the opponent is evading backwards (fig. 298). We follow this immediately using combination 10A (fig. 299), and execute a left back (straight) side kick 10 (fig. 300). We could also use combination 12A.

After the attack with R9, we complete the turning and start (fig. 301) with combination 8A. Here, we perform a high left front roundhouse kick 8 (fig. 302). We could also use combinations 2A, 4A, or 6A.

303

304

305

306

307

To fig. 303–305: Series L10+11A

The opponent is evading attack L10 with a step backward (fig. 303). We start with combination 11A (fig. 304) and execute a right high back (reverse) roundhouse kick 11. At the same time, we control the opponent's guard with the hand to be used for punching in the follow-up (fig. 305). We could also use 9A in the same way.

To fig. 303, 306–307: Series L10+7A

During the touchdown of our striking foot, we turn toward the opponent and start with combination 7A (fig. 306). We execute a high right front reverse round-house kick 7 (fig. 307). Similarly, we could use combinations 1A, 3A, or 5A.

308

309

310

311

312

To fig. 308–310: Series R11+8A

The opponent is evading our high back (reverse) roundhouse kick R11 with a step backward (fig. 308). We complete the turn and start with combination 8A (fig. 309), executing here a high front straight roundhouse kick 8 (fig. 310). Here, we could also use 2A, 4A, and 6A.

To fig. 308, 311–312: Series R11+12A

The striking foot lands in such a way that we can start with a fighting variation of combination 12A (fig. 311) and perform a high back (straight) reverted roundhouse kick 12 (fig. 312). Likewise, we could also use 10A.

153

313

314

315

To fig. 313–315: Series L12+11A

The opponent has evaded our high back (straight) reverted roundhouse kick with a step backward (fig. 313). After our striking foot lands, we start the combination 11A (fig. 314) and execute a high right back (reverse) roundhouse kick. We control the opponent's guard with the same hand we will use to follow-up with a punch (fig. 315). Similarly, we could also use combinations 1A, 3A, 5A, 7A, or 9A.

Specialties

In an ideal case, each fighter should be capable of linking all mutually linkable initiations, attacks, and finishing-off actions – intuitively and without hesitation, as the fighting situation demands each time.

In reality, however, one only can try to approach this ideal. The programmed schooling for sports fighting is meant to pass on to students, the basic techniques and tactics and the main possibilities for their uses. The students learn and practice the most commonly applied variations of basic fighting combinations. The more a student gradually masters the schooling program, the more his/her training becomes individualized. Over a period of time, each student finds out by him-/herself those combinations and their fighting variations which best suit him/her. He/she finds this out in training, and by gathering fighting experience in competitions, as well as by observing and analyzing the application of the various fighting combinations which other contestants prefer.

In time, some fighting combinations, which the fighter prefers, become his/her specialties. At this point, it is not important whether they have been picked out from the regular schooling program, taken over from other fighters, or created by themselves. The composition of one's own specialties depends on his/her mental and physical capabilities and traits: his/her height, body weight, anatomy and constitution, impulsiveness, reflexes, temperament, self-confidence, anxiety and aggression, fighting experience and state of fitness, etc. One fights in the same way as one generally behaves and moves. Some fighters intuitively choose frontal attacks, while others prefer attacks from the sides. Again, others feel more safe if they attack with a back kick and are capable of extremely fast spinning. None of the possible strategic concepts of fighting is universally better than any other. Each one has its own advantages and disadvantages, depending on how well it suits the particular fighter, and how useful it is in an actual fighting situation.

It is not enough to learn a smooth sequence of selected attacks. A specialty means much more. Only those single attacks or combinations can be called specialties, which one is able to perform from practically any position, with several varieties of initiations, continuations, and finishing-off actions, as the situation demands.

Particular fighting combinations, in which some fighters specialize, can gradually come to be used by other fighters also. Some become so widely known that they even are included in schooling programs. As students discover new possibilities and create new combinations, some of the old ones can, on the other hand, gradually fade from general usage. In this way, the creative power of individuals constructively participates in the further development and modernization of sports karate.

Jump Attacks

Because of their particular image, within and without karate circles, jump attacks deserve a separate and special mention.

Jump attacks represent, to the general public and especially to the unskilled beginners or uncritical admirers of karate, one of the main attractions of karate and related martial arts. There is a plethora of movies – beginning with "Easterns" from Hong Kong, Taiwan, and Korea – full of more or less convincing scenes with virtually acrobatic fights, and these have contributed substantially to such an attitude. However, they convey a mistaken idea that a fighter is better the more he/she can apply all those acrobatic "salto mortale" and other neck-breaking fighting skills – the higher the kick, the more turns in the air, the surer his/her success will be.

However, in practice the truth looks much different. Generally speaking, acrobatic jumps are rather rare in sports fights – even in karate related styles (e.g., taekwondo) where jump attacks are favored and highly rewarded.

Classic karate is, on the whole, rather ambivalent towards jump attacks. Most karate masters like to show-off with jump attacks, but at the same time, their fighting doctrine is based on techniques, where at least the whole of one foot is firmly planted on the ground. This doctrine also contradicts the judging practice in karate sports fights. In spite of the plethora of referees belonging to traditional styles, generally, successful jump attacks are rewarded.

There are some arguments against exercising jump attacks. First, it is obvious to anybody that it is relatively strenuous to master them. The logical conclusion is that they do not really pay off. With regard to the invested time and effort, their benefit is comparatively small. Further, the selection of technically possible and simultaneously tactically useful jump attacks is limited. From the tactical point of view, jump attacks are also risky, because the attacker is in an inferior position while in the air or landing. After jumping off, he/she can change neither the direction nor the type of attack, while the defender can detect the intent of his/her opponent at an early stage, thus being able to evade or even disturb the attacker while in the air. On landing, the attacker is in an obvious, predictable and relatively long state of reduced ability to start a new action (RAS) and is thus exposed to a counter-attack. (Compare table 5, p. 158)

However, in spite of these considerations, we should not simply avoid all use of jump attacks. In certain fighting situations, properly executed jump attacks can be very effective. This applies mostly in situations when we have surprised the opponent – just because of this kind of attack – and he/she has missed the opportunity for evasion or counter-attack.

Besides this, we see many attacks in sports fighting where both feet are in the air. This happens unintentionally most of the time and results either from vigorous, explosive starts or from interference by the opponent. For example, it occurs when a short fighter attacks the head of a taller one, or when an attack is being introduced with a leap. Spontaneous detachments from the ground happen because most jerky transfers of the body weight from one foot to the other, especially those including turning, are faster this way.

Apart from the practical reasons for learning jump attacks, there are also some didactic ones. Exercising attacks in the air, with no connection with the ground, accelerates the kinesthetic comprehension of those actions. Beyond that, continuous jumping strengthens the leg muscles and increases explosive strength, which is necessary for explosive starts, as well as endurance strength. (See table 5, p. 158)

The number of effective jump attacks is reasonably small. There are straight and reverse fist thrusts, strikes with the fist edge or back, reverse and straight thrust kicks, straight roundhouse kicks, the back (reverse) roundhouse kick, and the backward (straight) side kick. The photographs showing these jump attacks (see figs. 316–321, p. 159) have been taken as realistically as possible without using the usual advertising gimmicks, such as: frog perspective, not showing the ground, extremely low stance of the opponent etc. In this way, we wish to emphasize the real, practical usefulness of jump attacks.

Because they are very vulnerable to counter-attacks, it is meaningful to integrate the jump attacks into combinations. It is especially important to get ready for another start as fast as possible immediately after landing, so as to be able to continue with any further action necessary. A jump should therefore not distort our motor scheme to the degree that we are unable to start an action immediately afterward. This, however, is the main problem with jump attacks and can only be overcome with a proper understanding of their biomechanics, as well as persistent training.

Table 5: Characteristics of jump attacks

N e g a t i v e	P o s i t i v e
for training: − due to the high demand on coordination ability, they require a long training period to be mastered; − they give the false sense that with the height of the jump attack one improves his/her general fighting adeptness;	for training − they improve a fighter's general coordinative abilities, increase his/her pushing-off strength, and contribute to better and faster execution of the same techniques performed without jumping; − due to their attractiveness, they increase motivation for disciplined training, especially for beginners; − when mastered, they contribute to better self-assessment and consequently to increased self-confidence which further constitutes the main part of mental readiness for fighting;
for fighting − they are relatively slow and easily predictable; − it is relatively easy to evade them; − it is relatively easy to deflect them; − they make the fighter susceptible to errors in his/her balance; − they are unreliable in targeting vital points; − it is difficult to control the force of their impact.	for fighting − they contribute to psychological advantage, because they make a strong impression, especially on the audience, but also on referees and novices in sports fighting; − when used in surprise attacks, they are very effective; − they also happen spontaneously, especially in vigorously initiated attacks.

316 *Jumped straight fist thrust A1
(oi-tobi-tsuki)*

317 *Jumped reverse fist thrust A2
(gyaku-tobi-tsuki)*

318 *Jumped straight roundhouse
kick R8 (oi-mawashi-tobi-geri)*

319 *Jumped straight thrust kick L4
(oi-mae-tobi-geri)*

Fig. 316–321: Examples of jump attacks

These photographs have been taken as realistically as possible, i.e., intentionally without using the usual advertising gimmicks, such as; frog perspective, not showing the ground, extremely low stance of the opponent etc.

320 *Jumped back (reverse) roundhouse kick R11 (ushiro-mawashi-
tobi-geri)*

321 *Jumped back (straight) side kick
R10 (yoko-ushiro-tobi-geri)*

AFTERWORD

This rounds off the presentation of our fighting repertoire of sports karate. Yet, within the framework of this book, it has not been possible to include also a description of the method by which this repertoire can be learned. That subject is rather comprehensive and requires a voluminous book by itself. Here, we can only deal with the subject in brief outline.

The corresponding teaching method is called the *'direct'* method. The notion – direct – refers here to its exclusive orientation toward sports fighting, i.e., from the very beginning to the end of the schooling program. The related fighting repertoires, such as kata, breaking, self-defense, etc., are included only at a rather late stage, close to the black belt standard, largely to satisfy the curiosity of students, and to expand and enrich their kinetic experience.

Regarding the development of the motor capacity, specific for sports fighting, a beginner will become gradually acquainted with each one of the single combinations presented in this book, but in a backward sequence – that is, completely opposite to the way of teaching in traditional methods. First, one tries out the impact position, that is, the position of the whole body at the moment of hitting a vital point. Then, and only then, one learns all the previous stances and motions – which lead to that impact – phase by phase backwards. In this way, one knows all the following phases already when trying the complete combination for the first time from the starting position. With this approach, we create two effects which substantially accelerate the learning process, even with the most complex combinations. First, the backward learning of motions and stances requires, and, concomitantly produces the correct comprehension of the combination. Second, all unnecessary breaks, which otherwise distort the kinesthetic feeling and prolong the learning process, can be avoided in this way from the very beginning.

Once technically understood, the new combination is then exercised in gradually ever more complex and uncertain tactical situations - a small number of which have been shown in this book. In this way, the transition from the schooling exercise to the actual sports combat happens step by step. The students exercise the most typical situations and their significant variations in order to be ready for most of the requirements of sports combat.

The organization of regular schooling by the direct method is divided into 12 classes of 16 training hours each. Each class finishes with an 8-hour compact seminar when the students are also tested for belts. There are 12 student degrees with

6 belt colors (white, yellow, orange, green, blue, brown), finishing, of course, with a black belt.

In the higher classes of the schooling program, students gradually become involved in public sports contests, thus collecting practical experience regarding "real" sports fighting as well as the specifics of the corresponding training. After reaching the black belt, an alumni or alumna is ready to begin his/her actual contest career. Consequently, his/her training regimen will change substantially.

The quality of fighters at national and international karate sports fighting contests reached a rather high level long ago. Compared to 15 years or more ago, nowadays one cannot just walk in to a significant karate championship directly from any kind of sparring exercises, this mostly meaning a "light" fight *(randori)*. Whatever karate style-schooling a contestant has completed, at this level he/she is advised to follow a carefully designed periodic training scheme – as usual in other sports – if he/she wants to be successful. The periodization depends on the selected competitions in which he/she decides to participate. The content of periodic training should include special exercises for improving co-ordination, flexibility, speed, strength, endurance, and mental abilities. These special exercises must be properly timed and apportioned with regard to each other. This also applies as well to the technical and tactical training needed in a particular period.

However, a book, dealing exhaustively with all components of periodic training for karate sports contestants, has yet to be written.[22]. There are many excellent fighters and trainers around the globe who are applying the elements of periodic training and also demonstrating peak results, and from whom such a contribution could be expected. There are also various research projects on karate completed at several academic institutions. What is missing is a common orientation of the hitherto sporadic endeavors. To this end, a generally acceptable definition of karate as a global sport is needed. Such a conceptual clarification can be expected – in the long term – from the institutional unification – an unavoidable process in the development of karate as an Olympic sport. Let us hope so – actively.

NOTES

1) Let us not forget that this book was originally published in German in 1988, i.e., 10 years before the first English edition. However, the conditions on the book market (at least in Germany), and the characteristics and features of karate books since then have not changed much. Today, more than a decade later, although there is much more collected experience available, it is hard to find karate books which have achieved sufficient critical distance to the issues which crop up ad infinitum. It seems that karate's closely related discipline, taekwondo, has, in this respect, taken the lead with the book by Willy Pieter and John Heijmans, *Scientific Coaching for Olympic Taekwondo*, Meyer & Meyer, Aachen, 1997. Because of its clearly Western approach to taekwondo – based on extensive academic research – that book is most unusual in martial arts circles. It can also serve as a general guideline to karate trainers who wish to improve training of their top contestants, and especially to those who aspire to write a corresponding text book. In contrast to that, however, this book deals with a basic repertoire of karate techniques and tactics to be taught to students in a regular schooling program on the way to their black belts, and serves as groundwork for their later competitive careers.

2) Kinesiology includes several approaches to dealing with human motions – morphological, functional, empirical-analytical, and biomechanical. For more on the subject, see Klaus Willimczik/ Klaus Roth, *Bewegungslehre* (Kinesiology), Rowohlt, Reinbek bei Hamburg, 1987.

3) Similar coding, unavoidable in any serious attempt to modernize karate, has already been used by Japanese masters living in Europe (Chojiro Tani and Yoshinao Nambu).

4) A good example of this appears in Wolf-Dieter Wichmann, *Richtig Karate 2 – Kampftechniken* (Karate Correct 2 – Fighting Techniques), Munich, 1982, Chapter "Spezielle Kampfsituationen" (Special Fighting Situations).

5) Compare Gichin Funakoshi, Karate-Do: *My Way of Life*, Kodansha International, Tokyo, New York, San Francisco, 1975, pp. 33, 84. In his main work, *Karate-Do Kyohan: The Master Text*, Kodansha, Tokyo, New York San Francisco, 1973, Funakoshi reports about his first book Ryukyu Kempo: Karate, in which he, for the first time in 1922, presented karate to the general Japanese public. The same book was published in a revised edition a year later under the title Rentan Goshin Karate-Jitsu. According to Funakoshi, this was the first book on karate ever. However, this book has certainly ended the era of karate as a secret Okinawan martial art, and initiated its transformation into a popular combat sport.

6) Cit. Funakoshi, 1975, p. 36.

7) Cf. Elke von Oehsen, *Feudalistische Strukturen im Karate und ihre Auswirkungen in einer demokratischen Gesellschaft* (Feudal Structures in Karate and their Impacts on Democratic Societies). Paper presented on a conference in Trier, 13–14 January, 1990. To acquire a good overview of the historic origins of karate, see among others a book by Bruce A. Haines, *Karate's History and Traditions*, Ch. E. Tuttle, Ruthland, Tokyo, 1968.

8) Deficiencies in the schooling method of traditional karate are described by Jan Safr, a black belt second degree in shotokan, and a graduate in physical education. He wrote an extensive article, *"Ansätze einer neuen Karate-Methodik"* (Approaches to a New Karate Method) in the journal *Hochschulsport (University Sport)*, published by the General German University Sports Union, Darmstadt, 2/85. Among other things, he states in his critical analysis, that traditional karate eventually also gets some good results. However, the best students are successful, thanks to their personal natural endowments and strength which help them to compensate for the flawed training method. They eventually become good fighters, not because of their training, but in spite of it. Safr recommended some radical changes in the method of karate schooling. But he is only one out of many. Within the last 25 years or more, an array of new non-traditional, non-Eastern styles or schools of karate have appeared across Europe, America, and other continents, generated by the same kind of motivation as Jan Safr's. Some of them are described by Peter Lewis in his book, *The Way to the Martial Arts*, Exeter Books, New York, 1986, Chapter: Modern Eclectic Systems of Martial Arts.

9) Albrecht Pflüger, *Karate – ein fernöstlicher Kampfsport* (Karate – a Far Eastern Combat Sport), Falken, Wiesbaden, (w/o year), Vol. I and II.

10) Kurt Meinel, *Bewegungslehre*: Versuch einer Theorie der sportlichen Bewegungen unter pädagogischem Aspekt (Kinesiology – A Theoretical Approach to Motions in Sports from a Pedagogic Point of View), Volk und Wissen, Berlin, 1972, 5th edition (first edition 1960).

11) Concerning this statement, there has been some disagreement expressed by those who see in the traditional Budo-Karate an all-encompassing, universal way of personality improvement. They mean that this statement reduces karate to pure physical skill. However, let me emphasize that I have observed only the technical and tactical dimensions of karate fighting.

12) For more on all-encompassing regulations as a feature of sport, see Helmut Digel, "Wie die Vielfalt des Sports zusammenhängt" (How the Varieties of Sports are Interdependent), in H. Digel, *Lehren im Sport: Ein Handbuch für Sportstudierende und Übungsleiter* (Teaching in Sport: A Text-Book for Students of Sports and Instructors), Rowohlt, Reinbeck bei Hamburg, 1983; also in H. Digel, *Sport verstehen und gestalten* (Understanding and Shaping the Sport), Rowohlt, Reinbeck bei Hamburg, 1982.

13) See also Nikola Kurelic, *Osnovi sporta i sportskog treninga* (Basics of Sport and Sports Training), Sportska Knjiga, Beograd, 1967, p. 7.

14) Under the term "playful violence," Erich Fromm understands the motivation for engaging in "fighting games" such as zen-buddhist fencing or the war games of primitive tribes. In such games, it is not meant to kill someone, even though it might happen if, by his own mistake, the opponent "stands on the wrong spot." The leading motivation is to test one's fighting abilities, the mastering of combat skills, rather than to injure the opponent. However, there might be, subconsciously, some components of a destructive aggressiveness present. See Erich Fromm, *The Heart of Man*, (Chapter II: Different Forms of Violence), Harper & Row, New York, 1968, pp. 24–25.

15) Drago Ulaga, *Teorija telesne vzgoje in sportnega traniranja* (Theory of Physical Education and Sports Training), University of Ljubljana, 1959, p. 37.

16) Compare also Janko Leskosek, *Teorija fizicke kulture* (Theory of Physical Culture), Partizan, Beograd, 1971, p. 84.

17) More to that in Kurt Dieter, Ernst Dieter Rossmani, *"Freude am Sport – in Kooperation und Konkurenz"* (Joy in Sports – in the Co-operation and Competition), in H. Digel, op. cit., 1983.

18) A very enlightening illustration of this gives a comparison of statistical observations as to which and what kind of techniques (i.e., attacks) are primarily used in Japanese or European tournaments. See Teruo Kono, elke von Oehsen, *Karate: Training, Technik, Taktik*, Rowohlt, reinbeck bei Hamburg, 1968, Chapter "Wettkampfbeobachtungen" (Observation of Contests). The authors comment that the Japanese use less, and simpler techniques than Europeans because they fight using the one-point rules (shobu-ippon), and prefer consequently to play on certainty.

19) Bending, as the initiation of punching, refers to a complex of moves. It is named after the most obvious part of it: the arms are moving similar to bending a bow before releasing an arrow. Of course, it is not just arms which are moving, but the whole upper part of the body. Actually, the arms are only following the movement of the shoulders, and they follow the movement of the hips. The same sequence applies with the movement in the opposite direction. The launching of a hand thrust begins with a sudden move forward of the hip at the striking side, followed by a move of the same shoulder to which then the extension of the arm is added. This whiplash back-and-forward movement of the striking side of the body is known in sports theory under notions "eccentric-concentric contraction", "stretch-shortening cycle", or also as "plyometric effect." It is generally known that explosive moves in sports are exploiting the plyometric effect, also in cases when this is not very much in evidence. Karate can be no exception in this regard. Regretfully, there has hardly been any research completed in this field which could be applied as support to our descriptions. A good review on plyometrics is given by James C. Radcliffe and Robert C. Farentinos, *Plyometrics – Explosive Power Training*, Human Kinetics Publishers, Champaign, 1985.

20) The tension of a bending can be maximized when initiated as follows: (1) by first turning the heel of the foot opposite to the striking side inwards – when bending for a straight (same-sided) strike, or (2) by first turning the heel of the foot on the striking side outwards and up – when bending for a reverse (diametrical) strike.

21) When learning punches, it makes sense to work on the bending in its complete, maximum form and as thoroughly as possible. Once we have mastered bending to the full, we can then, in less favorable circumstances of a sports combat, easily apply it in any more or less reduced way required. Were we, instead, to exercise it from the start in reduced form we would not be able to increase its efficiency in moments when favorable, close-to-optimum chances arose.

22) Periodization of training is not yet popular in karate. However, it is an inavoidable result of any consequent analysis of the goals and aims of karate sports training. The contribution of W. Pieter and J. Heimans (op. cit., Endnote 1, pp. 46 et seq), a good example to be followed, has nicely demonstrated that in the field of taekwondo.

LIST OF FIGURES AND TABLES

ABOUT THE AUTHOR

Dr. Rudolf Jakhel, born 1942, presently a karate black belt seventh degree (FEKDA), studied in Ljubljana (Slovenia) and Aachen (Germany). After receiving his doctoral degree in economics and social sciences in 1975, he lived and worked as a researcher, university teacher, and development consultant in Germany, Slovenia, the USA, and in Guyana (South America).

He started practicing karate in 1968 in Stuttgart, Germany. Later, while living in Slovenia (then a part of the former Yugoslavia), he learned several karate styles – shotokan, shitoryu, shukokai, and sankukai – and was a successful contestant. In 1971, he became the federal vice-champion in the open category, and won, as a member of the national team, the third prize at the EKU European Championship in Paris. Thereafter, after moving to Germany, he became active as a federal referee, trainer and adviser to the technical commission in the Karate Section of the German Judo Union – in those times the strongest German karate federation. He also took over as mentor to students of sport specializing in karate at the Institute of Sports Science, University of Technology, Aachen.

The problem of teaching karate at an academic institution motivated him to undertake extensive research on the possibilities of rationalization in karate. He kept working on this project wherever he lived. Considering sports fighting as the very didactic objective in sports karate, he eventually developed a non-style, direct teaching method. His ideas have been accepted in various countries, especially by university karate circles.

Currently, Dr. Jakhel is heading the Combat Sports Program at the Faculty of Sports, University of Ljubljana, and is in charge of karate within the University Students Sports Union of Slovenia. Besides this, he is also technical director of the Modern Sports Karate Associates International (MSKAI), Luxembourg, chief instructor of MSKA Germany, and member of the technical commission in the European Federation of Associated Karate Disciplines (FEKDA), Milan, Italy.